Drink More Whiskey

DRINK MORE WHISKEY

EVERYTHING YOU NEED TO KNOW ABOUT YOUR NEW Favorite DRINK!

 DANIEL YAFFE

ILLUSTRATIONS BY

MARY KATE McDEVITT

CHRONICLE BOOKS
SAN FRANCISCO

To my (older) brother Jonathan,
who will eventually learn to love whiskey.

Library of Congress Cataloging-in-Publication Data available.

ISBN 978-1-4521-0974-9

Manufactured in China

Designed by Alice Chau
Illustrations by Mary Kate McDevitt

10 9 8 7 6 5 4 3 2 1

Chronicle Books LLC
680 Second Street
San Francisco, California 94107
www.chroniclebooks.com

CONTENTS

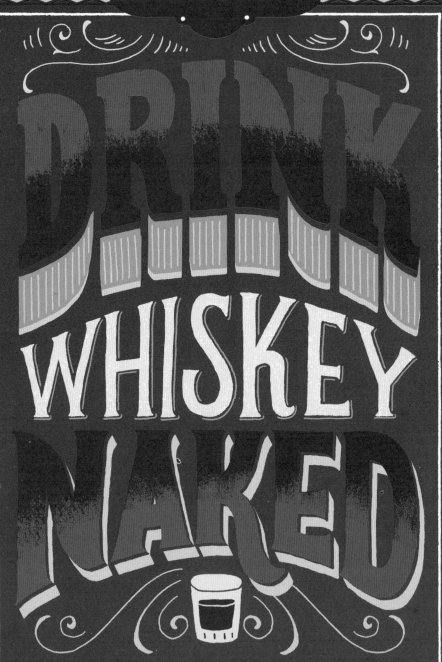

DRINK WHISKEY NAKED

This is not your granddaddy's whiskey book. It is a book for a new generation of whiskey drinkers. I don't mean eighteen-year-olds who are raiding their parents' liquor cabinet or frat boys who are celebrating their twenty-first birthday. I mean anyone who has fallen in love with the food revolution and liquefied it. This is for folks who are looking to drink better whiskey and attempt to understand it.

Back in the golden days, my grandfather had his CANADIAN CLUB whisky and would drink it the same way whenever he decided to reach for the bottle: a whiskey sour before his meat loaf or, on occasion, after a Jell-O salad. He was part of the old generation of drinkers. It was the generation that drank a Coke every day with lunch, ate spaghetti and meatballs every Wednesday night, and went to the local buffet every Tuesday.

That's not us. Our generation wants to know the next best thing. We're the sushi generation because we had never tasted anything like it, and we're at a new restaurant every chance we get. Never had Burmese food? Bring on the tea leaf salad. We're an eclectic and experimental bunch that marvels at international and local quality over familiar comfort. We're the generation that will change careers every five years, start up the company of our dreams, and wave to llamas on top of Machu Picchu. Whether you remember it or not, we are the generation that welcomed Harry Potter jelly beans in such flavors as grass, earwax, and dirt, knowing that the point wasn't to find your favorite flavor. The age of discovery has transformed into the age of sensory exploration.

We've finally stepped up from a low point on the American cultural palate. The 1970s and 1980s were marked by a surge of vodka consumption because people didn't want to taste their alcohol. Things are changing. Going out is no longer about super-sweet grenadine cocktails and soda-laced Long Island Iced Teas.

It's about fresh thyme and knowing the name of the cow whose carcass was made into the truffled meatball you're about to fork into your mouth. The mere fact that you've made it this far into the book means that you want to know more about whiskey. If you were just drinking to get buzzed, you could have already been shit-faced by now.

I've had an incredible whiskey journey chock-full of mind-blowing scenery and characters. I've visited more distilleries than I care to count, drank whiskey with distillers across the globe, and marveled as a 3-D drink became four-dimensional. That's what this book is about. Sitting with people who have made their livelihood from whiskey, I've geeked out about yeast strains, the genus of oak trees used to make barrels, and how best to cut peat from bogs on Islay. It's a trip to sit with a fifth-generation whiskey mogul and tell him that his Scotch tastes like rotten grass (to his delight). All of this has been a ton of fun—just the way drinking whiskey should be.

WHY ARE YOU READING THIS BOOK?

Millions of intimidated consumers feel as though they should open their mouths to drink whiskey rather than to ask questions about it. I believe it's time for a new discourse about the spirit. I did not write this book because I'm an expert on whiskey. There are hundreds of people who could teach a college-level course on the subject. But we need to take whiskey off of its throne and bring it onto the playground. I'm tired of pompous old men telling me how to drink whiskey: "Don't add water." "Add precisely two drops." "Don't ever mix this single malt." "You added *what* to it?" It's confusing and it's pretentious.

You don't need to know everything about every bottle. I'm giving you the background information so that you can go out and learn for yourself. If you step back from all the chemistry, tradition, rules, regulations, and names, whiskey is simple and can be enjoyed without an encyclopedia in hand. Too often it is enveloped in dusty rhetoric and esoteric jargon that does little more than prompt blank stares. When it stops being fun, put down your drink, go for a hike, and then reach for an iced tea.

I'm not saying that you should turn to whiskey for everything, but the beauty of the spirit is that, like music, there is a whiskey for nearly every occasion. Perhaps you sip on a LAPHROAIG single malt one evening before a warm fire and pour BULLEIT bourbon over ice on a warm summer afternoon. You might have your favorite brand to crack open at a wedding, and a different bottle to confide in after a breakup. **Ultimately, whiskey is a social drink; it always tastes better among friends.**

I'm intentionally breaking the code of conduct and talking about whiskey the way I would if we were friends hanging out at a bar. This book does not employ all the traditional terminology. It's here to help integrate whiskey into your life without having to spend a lifetime to learn every minute detail first. You don't need to be a mechanic to enjoy driving fancy cars. You're not a distiller and you'll never need to know the optimal temperature at which column stills operate or the genetic makeup of the barley in your favorite Scotch. So for now, just learn enough to know what the hell you're drinking and, more important, why you're drinking it.

A NOTE BEFORE YOU DIVE IN

The following chapters are not a reference guide. You can find handbooks on the shelves of bars and liquor stores and enough second- and third-hand volumes on eBay. Not every brand in the world is included in this book, and the ones that don't appear are not intentionally left out because I don't like them. I'm not going to list bottles for you and tell you a hundred times over that you're going to taste vanilla and oak in this bourbon and peat and ripe fruit in that Scotch. If that's the kind of information you're looking for, you're in luck, because enough budding whiskey critics exist to fill a small country. Whiskey drinkers love to vocalize their thoughts, and volumes have been written on nearly every bottle. Your goal shouldn't be to read through piles of CliffsNotes; instead, you should be writing your own. This book is a smattering of stories, history, anecdotes, and approachable ways to understand whiskey. It will help you visualize what you're drinking and bring cultural relevance to a bottle of booze. Use this book as a jumping-off point.

WHY WHISKEY?

Any way you drink it, whiskey is one of the world's most iconic spirits, with a tremendous character and history. It was there when the United States was fighting for independence. It has been poured down throats during celebrations and soirees and coveted during triumphant battles and historic moments. I can guarantee you that Winston Churchill wasn't downing shots of cherry vodka and doing sake bombs while sending his men into battle.

Whiskey is a cultural celebrity everywhere from China to Brazil. It stars in shows like *Boardwalk Empire* and *Mad Men*, is a favorite drink of Lady Gaga, and has been memorialized by authors Hunter S. Thompson and F. Scott Fitzgerald. It is poured in country songs and across hip-hop stages and has the kind of cultural cachet that the world hasn't seen since the Pet Rock craze of the mid-1970s. Starting to learn about whiskey can seem more daunting than trying to analyze nineteenth-century Russian literature. Begin by simply enjoying it. You probably didn't like your first beer, but if you're anything like me, you crossed that threshold long ago and are now reaching for double IPAs and Belgian tripels. Whiskey can take you on a similar ride.

Whiskey tasting is not trial and error. It's trial and trial again. It's a testament to the spirit that so many crazed whiskey fanatics are found around the globe. There are dozens of whiskey-only magazines and hundreds of elite clubs, blogs, Facebook fan groups, and Twitter feeds devoted to whiskey. I know more whiskey geeks than I know *Star Wars* geeks. But each and every whiskey savant went through a protracted process to get there. The more you taste, the more you know. **Great whiskey drinkers are made, not born.**

If you're not sure how to drink whiskey, drink it naked. At least no one will tell you that you're drinking it incorrectly.

BASICALLY

the

BASICS

I hated my first whiskey. I don't remember what it was and it doesn't really matter, but I think it made me sick. I was probably drunk at three o'clock in the morning in my friend's college dorm room, and it's not something I'd like to recall. Everyone has a story. The question I've heard a lot is what's a good whiskey? Or rather, what's the best whiskey? If my first whiskey made me sick, what's a good "smooth" whiskey that won't? Frankly, a good whiskey is one that you enjoy.

Many of the folks who have been working at distilleries their whole careers have plentiful answers for the curious consumer. As I toured the peat fields on Scotland's island of Islay with Iain McArthur, who has been a warehouseman at the LAGAVULIN distillery for more than forty years, he looked me in the eye and said, his thick Scottish accent at full throttle, "The best whisky is the one you get for free." Dozens of other Scotsmen have said, chuckling, that the best whisky is the one you've got in your hand. Hundreds of books are available to help you navigate the seemingly infinite library of whiskies that grows by the month. Dozens of competitions are popping up, judged by distillers, whiskey experts, and drinkers who have been tasting whiskies since before your mother was old enough to drink. These references can help direct your choices, but at the end of the day, it's really all about what fits your taste buds at this specific moment. Flavors and aromas can vary depending on what you just ate, where you are, or who you're with. The whiskey you drink on your wedding night might be the best-tasting whiskey you'll ever have.

The whiskey curriculum continues to grow. The industry is constantly changing and adapting, and there exists a breadth of knowledge thousands of bottles wide. I'm sifting through the bullshit for you so we can get right to the good stuff. Before you stick your head into a bucket of booze, here is the information that you will need to make the rest of the book more digestible. In order to break the rules, you must know what they are. Understanding this small foundation will take you a long way. It will be your Swiss Army knife for a whiskey journey that will span your entire life.

Remember, this is just a beginning.

WHICH WHISKEY IS WHICH

Whiskey is the overall category and can be made anywhere. Subcategories are defined by where the whiskey is made and what it is made from. All bourbon is whiskey. All Scotch is whiskey. All Canadian, Japanese, and Irish whiskies are also whiskey. These are just descriptions of where your whiskey was created. Drink rye? That's also a kind of whiskey. Here's a little chart to make the naming oh so obvious. It's totally acceptable to call any of these drinks whiskey, but if you order a whiskey at a bar, it could be any one of these. Whiskey, according to flavor, can mean a whole lot of different things.

YOU SAY POTATO(E)

For some reason, everyone gets caught up on the spelling of whiskey. It's utterly unimportant, and no one should spend more than thirty seconds on understanding the rule. Ireland and most U.S. distilleries spell it with the *e*, while Scotland, Japan, Canada, and most other countries spell it without the *e*. A few American distilleries, including **GEORGE DICKEL** and **MAKER'S MARK**, drop the *e* to confuse you. You don't get your arse all knotted up trying to analyse the British spelling of *flavours* and *colours*, so try to stay centred and know that we're all speaking the same language. For the sake of this book, when I'm talking about Scotch, Canadian, or Japanese *whisky*, I defer to their spelling, and when I talk about U.S. or Irish *whiskey* or *whiskey* in general, I use the U.S. spelling, unless, of course, we're talking about a U.S. brand that spells it without the *e*. That said, I don't want you to worry about spelling whiskey. Instead, worry about tasting it.

A BRIEF HISTORY

Each chapter chronicles the trajectory of whiskey, and each story is a puzzle piece that fits with others to form a complex and beautiful history. Before you dive into Whiskey 101, it's valuable to understand the basic story of how the spirit was born and why it became more popular than Pac-Man.

Distilling technology has been around for millennia and was originally used to make perfumes in the Middle East. In Europe, it was used to distill wine into spirits. The technology stayed in a religious realm and the knowledge spread from monastery to monastery. As the know-how made its way across the continent, God's men in Ireland decided to distill beer, since grain grew more easily there than the grapes used on the mainland. That was the birth of whiskey.

As the distilling process moved across the British Isles, it was taken up by small-scale farmers. Soon enough, royalty became interested and found they too were fond of the so-called water of life. From that moment on, the history of whiskey has been at the focal point of taxation issues. Its own trajectory was marred and shaped by government regulation and the balance of a thirsty world. Whiskey making thrived in Scotland and Ireland and spread to new shores with those who left to start new lives in colonial America. Techniques of the whiskey-making process changed as it hit the New World, and again whiskey was a key character in the political and social landscape of the emerging world power. It was sought by governing officials and western pioneers alike and became the drink of choice for hundreds of American senators, poets, and actors. Once the whiskey industry took hold in the United States, the rest of the world looked on with envy, and other countries leapt into making and consuming the spirit.

Somewhere along this time line, whiskey became a manly man drink and a symbol of complexity and masculinity. Things flipped on their head, and what was first made in monasteries and then on small farms is now produced by multinational companies that supply the world with enough whiskey to float on. Not many pastors make whiskey any more, but I've sure met a bunch who love drinking it.

WHISKEY MAKING IN ONE MINUTE

Although you don't need to know how to make whiskey to drink it, knowing the ABCs will help you understand what you're drinking and why it tastes the way it does. Any and all whiskey is simply distilled beer made from three ingredients: water, yeast, and grain. Every distillery makes its whiskey in essentially the same way, with the same kinds of equipment. Making it is a relatively simple process but a difficult one to master. The distiller takes cereal grains (namely corn, barley, oats, rye, or spelt, or some mix of grains, known as the mashbill), smashes them up, adds hot water and yeast, and lets the mixture ferment to make beer. The beer is then boiled in big stills. Since alcohol has a lower boiling point than water, the alcohol is captured as vapor and condensed back to liquid form. For some whiskies, this is repeated one or two more times. The alcohol is collected, put into barrels, and left to age until it is ready to drink. Luckily, there is no yellow dye no. 5 in whiskey; the wooden barrels give it its beautiful color, its oaky smell, and much of its taste. That's oversimplified, but it is nearly that simple.

Do the math: a whiskey that is 90 proof is 45 percent pure alcohol. That means that more than 50 percent is water and the rest is compounds that contribute flavor and color. Since pure alcohol and water don't taste like anything, it's that small percentage that you're most interested in tasting. A lot of time goes into making that 5 percent. When people talk about "smoothness," it is not about alcohol content; it's just a great 5 percent.

PROOF READING

Everyone wants to know a whiskey's strength. Although it shouldn't be of the utmost concern unless you're driving home after a few tastes, it's good to understand the "heat" of any whiskey. Most whiskies fall in the 80 to 90 proof range (40 to 45 percent alcohol), and you can find many that are significantly stronger. If a bottle is "cask strength," it means that the whiskey was not watered down and will pack a punch of around 120 proof (60 percent alcohol). Cask-strength whiskey is not always easy to sip on, and be careful when sticking your nose into it. Some cask-strength whiskies slide down without a burn, however, and can be enjoyed neat. When you taste, remember that "spicy" and "strong" are two different sensations in your mouth. A dram of whiskey might taste "harsh" because of its spiciness rather than its alcohol content.

HOW TO DRINK WHISKEY

Open your mouth, pour in whiskey, close mouth, and swallow. Repeat.

Whiskey companies should appropriate the 1990s Reese's peanut butter cup campaign slogan: There's No Wrong Way to Drink a Whiskey. If you're throwing down cash to buy a bottle of whiskey, you should enjoy it however the hell you want to: straight, with water, with ice, with juice, even with peanut butter and chocolate—do whatever suits you. The snobbery around whiskey is on its way out. **I'll walk you through the traditional ways of tasting and mixing whiskey and why they're recommended, but take them all with a grain of salt. Or two grains, if that's the way you like it.**

HOW TO TASTE WHISKEY

There's a difference between tasting whiskey and drinking it. You wouldn't taste a fine wine by first making sangria with it, or taste a fine cut of tuna belly by first boiling it and mixing it with mayonnaise to turn it into a tuna fish sandwich. Most people want to know how to taste whiskey—and the loose rules have been honed for years by distillers, connoisseurs, and bartenders trying to figure out how best to explore a diverse range of flavors on some common ground rules. Every time you drink whiskey you don't need to follow this step by step, but it's a good orientation. This is generally what people do, and why they do it.

First, relax. Take off your coat and put everything down. This is not a board meeting and you aren't about to walk into litigation. Make sure you're with friends or other human beings. Whiskey tasting should be social; doing it alone is never as much fun.

Stick your nose into your whiskey glass and smell it. Do it again. Try smelling from varying depths and places along the rim. Remember the smell and do it again. If you don't enjoy the aroma, that's a red flag. A whiskey's fragrance (or its "nose," if you prefer to use the lingo) can tell you a lot about the liquid. It's part of the experience and I've seldom loved a whiskey whose smell didn't intoxicate me first. Splash it around and stick your nose in it again. Pour a couple of drops into your hands, rub it around, and then smell it. You'll have evaporated the alcohol and should be able to smell the essence of the grain and essential oils more clearly. If you've found a smell you love, rub a bit of the eau-de-whiskey behind your ears and on your neck for maximum effect.

If you're out to taste whiskey, it's most beneficial first to try it neat, with nothing in it. It can be fiery and full of alcohol, but try it the way it was bottled. You can always add more to your glass, but it's impossible to take anything out of it. Sip on it and nurse it, that is, move the whiskey around your mouth. Take note of how it feels as it slides down your tongue and into your throat. Flavors can change in your mouth. That is part of the experience. Breathe out and taste it. There's nothing wrong with having a beer at your side to keep you company and bring your taste buds back to familiarity. It's not a race. Although I've had friends who think that their whiskey snifter is just a top shelf shooter of Scotch, that surely wasn't the experience the distiller imagined when the spirit was being made.

No need to swirl around the whiskey to mimic a hyperactive wine taster. That will actually kick up the alcohol vapor and make the whiskey more difficult to smell. It might look badass to wrap your fingers around your glass so your hand warms up the whiskey, but it will have the same effect and evaporate the alcohol. If you need something to do between sips, tilt your glass a bit and slowly turn it to check out the color and oiliness of the whiskey. It's mesmerizing and will make you look like an expert.

Try a few whiskies in the same sitting. When you're just starting out, you've got very little to compare. **Having a few tastes side by side will not only give you a frame of reference but will also help you taste through a range of flavors and get your tongue dancing.** It will make it easier to sense what you like and what rubs you the wrong way.

Next, add a little water and taste the whiskey again. **Water is to whiskey what oxygen is to wine: it will help open the flavors and bring out new smells that you otherwise won't pick up.** If you must use an eyedropper to measure your water precisely, please don't do it in public. It might get the approval of the old man in the kilt watching over you, but it's ridiculous and pretentious. You can use a straw as a pipette if you need to add a few drops, but remember this is not a science lab. Add more water if you want to. Distillers add water to most whiskies right before they're bottled anyhow. It's fine to keep adding water until you taste flavors that you like. Just make sure you're using decent water. It would be a shame for you to ruin the taste of a fine whiskey by using chlorinated or contaminated tap water.

If you like tasting whiskey cold, feel free to throw in some ice (the larger the chunk the better, as it will melt more slowly). Unless you want a glass full of water that tastes like whiskey, don't get a cup full of ice and add a shot of whiskey—use just a cube or two. The cold will mask some flavors but bring out others. A few companies are now marketing whiskey stones: rock cubes or disks that you freeze and drop into your whiskey to chill it without watering it down. Since water can bring some nice changes to whiskey, I've never gravitated toward whiskey stones, but they are a cool addition to your home bar. If you love whiskey paraphernalia, there is no harm in testing them out. The folks at the LAPHROAIG distillery in Scotland even told me of some die-hard fans who picked up rocks on the beach outside the distillery to use as their own whiskey stones.

If you feel like tasting whiskey while eating chocolate or pairing it with food, that's another great way to take your taste buds on a trip. After all, whiskey tasting is a big roller-coaster ride that's not always about getting to the finish line.

Don't hesitate to put whiskey away for a while. It won't change in the bottle, but your palate will. What you like today might strike you differently tomorrow, and what you really enjoyed last month might taste like an astringent medicine next week.

A great way to taste a tremendous amount of whiskey is to get together with friends, have a whiskey potluck, and taste your way around the table. Record your thoughts so you'll remember what you've had. You can either reach for a pen and paper or download a whiskey app on your phone. After tasting twenty whiskies, I rarely remember two of them if I have failed to take notes.

BLING BLING

Perhaps the second most confusing thing about whiskey after the spelling is the price. Some bottles are dirt cheap and others sell on eBay for about what you would spend on a flight from London to Hawaii. The big questions are about the differences in brands and how to navigate them. I can tell you from the start that some modestly priced bottles are delicious, and that I've had glasses of

Scotch twenty times the price that I would never order a second time. It all depends on why you're drinking it. Are you ordering a glass to impress a boss? A cheap well shot probably won't get you a raise. On the other hand, if you're making a big vat of whiskey sours for a summer potluck, filling it with premium, expensive bottles of single malt isn't the best use of your money. Before you drop your weekly salary on a whiskey, you might want to think if you'd rather have three times as much of the less pricey bottle.

It's important to understand what makes some whiskies expensive. The first factor is age. Not because older is necessarily better, but because as whiskey ages, a large percentage of the alcohol evaporates. Since distilleries then have less to sell, they need to charge more to recoup their costs. The longer a whiskey ages, the more time it takes up space in a warehouse—another expense that gets tacked onto the price.

The second cost factor is all about how much whiskey is made and how much still exists. A single malt from Scotland's **PORT ELLEN** distillery that shut down in 1983 is destined to be expensive (and probably a solid investment). This consideration is simple supply-and-demand economics. The quantity is limited because the distillery no longer exists and its whisky is coveted among collectors. Similarly, microdistilleries make such small quantities that their prices are higher (than those of large international companies) to cover their cost per bottle.

The third factor that determines cost is plain and simple marketing: expensive brands for the sake of being flashy and high prices for perceived age and quality. There is a time and place for these bottles, as well. Buying a bottle to kiss up to someone who doesn't know a thing about whiskey? I guarantee that the bottle with the big price tag on the top shelf will be impressive.

WHAT IS MALT?

The term *malt* has become shorthand for single-malt Scotches and in general refers to malted barley. As a verb, malting is the process of tricking barley (or other grains) into thinking that it's springtime by soaking it in water. Each of the kernels starts to sprout and they are heated up (or smoked—think peated whiskey) to stop them from growing into full plants. The sprouted barley is then thrown into the whiskey-making process. If the initial steps of making beer go sour, it can be turned into malt vinegar, a perfect condiment for fish and chips. When you malt a grain, it changes its starches and makes it ideal for creating alcohol. If a bottle says anything about malt, it's made entirely with malted grains, and in Scotland, it will always be malted barley.

SINGLE MALT VERSUS SINGLE BARREL VERSUS SMALL BATCH

Single malt is a reference to both how and where a whiskey is made, and *single barrel* and *small batch* refer to which whiskey is actually put into a bottle. These classifications get confused all the time.

A single malt is a whiskey that comes from a single distillery and is made from 100 percent malted grain (99 percent of the time we're talking about malted barley). A single malt can be made from a mix of different barrels, but you still know where the whiskey was made, who made it, and you could go visit its birthplace. Single malts can be made anywhere in the world, but single-malt Scotch is the standard bearer.

On the other hand, a single barrel is just that. In fact, it could be called a one barrel. Whiskey goes into a wooden barrel, ages for a specified number of years, and then goes into a bottle.

It is never mixed with other barrels of whiskey. You know single barrels are usually good because they are hand selected and tasted for quality. Every major whiskey country is making some sort of single-barrel whiskey. You know where it was made, what it was made from, and who made it. It could be single-barrel bourbon, single-barrel Irish whiskey, or single-barrel single malt. If you fall in love with a single barrel, jot down the specific barrel number (look for it on the label) and go back to where you bought it. You might just be able to get another bottle from the same barrel. Another bottle from a different barrel could taste completely different. **Although there is usually some consistency among single barrels from a distillery, they can be an exciting whiskey grab bag.**

Small batch is a marketing term that doesn't have a hard-and-fast meaning. Usually it's a premium whiskey made in a smaller quantity (and therefore more expensive) than a standard bottling and made from barrels that hold the best-tasting whiskey. Any kind of whiskey can be made in small batches.

PERCEPTION

Whiskey tasting is all about perception. It's like lightly crossing your eyes and staring at a Magic Eye image and then chatting with your friend about what you see. I might love a Scotch that you hate, or the Irish whiskey I just enjoyed might sit like a grass-flavored jelly bean in your mouth. And that's perfectly okay. Let your mind run wild. No whiskey actually has cinnamon, vanilla, fruit, or grass in it, but it's still a fun goal to search for subtle flavors. It makes tasting whiskey a dynamic experience. Be specific. What does it mean to taste mint? Is it fresh spearmint, or a red-and-white candy mint? The sweetness of crème brûlée is quite different from the sweetness of a ripe apple. Think for a second about Big Red gum. Does just thinking about it hit your tongue in a specific place? If I told you something tasted like cinnamon, I could be talking about several different flavors; on the other hand, Big Red strikes a distinctive chord. A friend of mine tried a Scotch that reminded him of sitting on sterile paper in a doctor's office while dressed in an open-back hospital gown. Although no one loves the drafty one-size-fits-all outfits, I knew exactly what smell he was talking about—and I had to try it. Anything goes. Some Scotch distillers even have a flavor thesaurus sitting on their desk with entries like child's vomit and electric cables. Everything your tongue senses is fair game. Just remember that "smooth" is not a taste.

The beauty of sipping whiskey with friends, family, and complete strangers is realizing that though you weren't thinking about it, your bourbon actually does taste like a Werther's Original. I have only one tongue, so I can't taste everything a whiskey has to offer. How utterly boring would it be if we all had the same sense of taste? "I taste apricot fruit leather." "Yep, me too." "This is my favorite." "Yep, agreed."

Even within your own mouth, perception can make whiskey tasting into a series of funhouse mirrors. Just like brushing your teeth makes the freshest orange juice taste like a rancid toilet cleaner, flavors in whiskey can be flipped upside down by what you're eating, drinking, or smoking.

Cigars and whiskey seem to go together like Bonnie and Clyde. There's now even a magazine called *Cigars & Spirits* to talk through the pairing. Light one up and grab a dram if you want to feel like you just sold your company, but it's mostly about the image. The cigar will trick your tongue and bring out the sweeter nuances of a whiskey, but keep puffing away and you're likely not to taste a whole lot in your glass.

WHERE TO BUY WHAT

You don't have to run to a fancy liquor store to find great whiskey. A lot of brands are common anywhere. Try whiskey everywhere. Even Costco's Kirkland-branded whiskies turn up some surprises (they are made by large whiskey companies that make other big-name brands). International bar scenes will carry a whole collection of different whiskies. Many companies release brands only in specific regions. Duty-free shops are often fantastic places to have a few sips before cramming your legs into a 747. Not only have I been to airports that have whiskey experts pouring me tastes of every bottle before eight o'clock in the morning, but often companies will make special editions that are sold only at duty-free shops. More websites are selling whiskey online, and if they navigate the legalities just right, they are fantastic resources for finding less-common bottles. Ask a lot of questions; even your local bartender might have some surprises for you.

RESOURCES

Thanks to millions of fanatic aficionados, volumes on whiskey have emerged from every corner of the globe: thousands of blogs, hundreds of books, several big magazine titles, and more information than most brains can reasonably handle. A lot of the books offer listings of whiskies with the author's notes about each one. Michael Jackson was not just the king of pop. Another Michael Jackson, the king of whiskey, might perhaps have been the most prolific whiskey writer the world will ever know. Whiskey geeks will often use his books or Jim Murray's *Whisky Bible* as a checklist of labels to try. I have even seen tourists at distilleries marking whiskies off of a piece of paper as if they were birders competing to update their life list.

These books have thousands of reviews and descriptions that may serve as a platform to understand whiskey, but they stop there. Just because Michael Jackson loved MACALLAN 25 doesn't mean you should go buy ten bottles of it. I don't read tomes about a painting before I look at it, and it is often best to dive into whiskey first and ask questions later. Sometimes tasting notes don't mean much at all. In his *Whisky Bible*, Jim Murray explained a PORT CHARLOTTE six-year-old Scotch as a proverbial orgasm. With a nose of "Ohhhhh . . . arrrrrrghh . . . mmmmmmmm . . . oh, the peat, the peat . . . yessssss . . . oh my god . . . , mmmmmm . . . ohhhhhh . . . ," his explanation is a flowing river of literary orgasmic moans. Sure, orgasms are delicious, but that's most likely not what you'll get when you throw down your entire wallet for a bottle. Take reviews as walking sticks; you'll have to do most of the hiking yourself. The famous names and icons lend legitimacy to brands and are flaunted in marketing material everywhere. For example, many people were hesitant about diving into a whiskey from India until Jim Murray raved about AMRUT in a review. You don't have to love what the experts love and, ultimately, your best guides will be your own senses and the people around you. In other words, look to your coworkers, family members, favorite bartenders, or Facebook friends for recommendations. Want to dive into more literature? Check out the bibliography at the end of this book. If you're inspired to geek out with other human beings in real life, join a whiskey club—or better yet, start your own.

———

Now that you know the rules, you can break them and go explore.

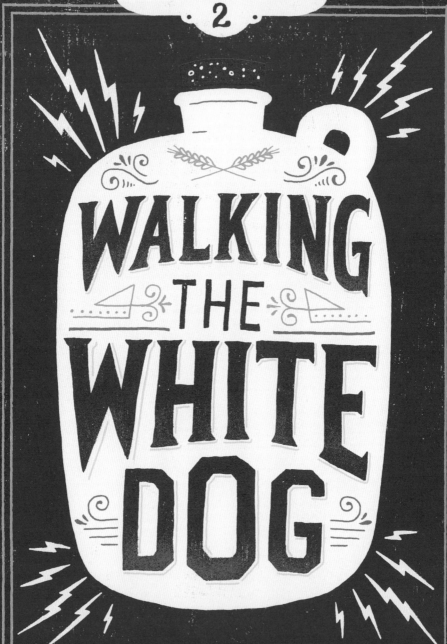

CHAPTER 2

WALKING THE WHITE DOG

White dog is a great place to start any whiskey journey. Also known as white whiskey or green whiskey, white dog is more properly called *new make* in the United Kingdom (make sure you raise your pinkie when you say that). But whatever name you choose to call it, it is simply any newborn, unaged whiskey. It hasn't matured in the wooden barrel that gives it a golden color and much of its famous whiskey flavor. Every whiskey from the smokiest Scotch to the most obscure Japanese single malt started off as a clear new make—or rocket fuel as the Aussies call it.

Beyond the fact that white dog is perhaps the simplest, rawest, and purest spirit among whiskies, we're starting here because it has no rules. You don't need to assess its color or learn how to pronounce its name. Nor do you need to put on your kilt or sip it in the proper fashion. After all, white dog and its historically illegal twin, moonshine, are the spirits of breaking rules. It's what new Scottish and Irish immigrants created when they first set up shop in the United States. It's what bayonet-wielding workers were drinking on the run in the 1790s when they launched the Whiskey Rebellion, America's first large uprising. It's what hillbillies soaked up in Appalachia while snuggling with their cousins, and what bootleggers packed in unmarked bottles and mustached, speakeasy bartenders poured behind closed doors during Prohibition. It's the renegade spirit of Al Capone.

During Prohibition, unaged whiskey was cheap, fast, and easy to get around (which is why it's also called white lightning). Instead of storing the freshly distilled booze in oak barrels and watching it age to become a proper whiskey, bootleggers bottled it right away and sold it for a slick buck, before the feds knew what was happening. With desperation for a buzz in the air, distillers didn't care much about the quality and imbibers didn't have high expectations for its taste. As a result, the whiskey was harsh and impure—the kind of alcohol that smacks you in the face. Not surprisingly, this gave unaged whiskey a bad name and scarred the cultural memories for generations to come. Speakeasies across the country would often mask the rough flavor with a strong mixer—think ginger ale, bitters, or juice.

Moonshiners would modify the mechanics of their cars so they could outdrive the feds and get white dog to thirsty consumers. What started as a necessary means to deliver hooch turned competitive, and drivers banded together in the beginnings of what is today one of the most widely watched sports in the world: NASCAR racing. After Prohibition, drivers came together in Daytona Beach, Florida, to continue the tradition and institutionalize the sport. Junior Johnson, a member of the NASCAR Hall of Fame, started out as a moonshiner and rumrunner in the South. He won dozens of races in his career, but only after spending almost a year behind bars for getting caught working at his father's moonshine distillery. Known as the man who invented the bootleg, a high-speed 180-degree turn to avoid the feds, Johnson is now partial owner of **PIEDMONT DISTILLERS**, maker of Midnight Moon liquor, which is marketed as the Johnson family's own moonshine recipe. Although the lore of illegal moonshine dates back to colonial days, you had better believe that people across the country continue making and selling illicit whiskey. By some estimates, more than seven thousand unauthorized distilleries remain in operation in the United States.

The most famous contemporary moonshiner was a gentle Southerner named Popcorn Sutton. As one rung in generations of backwoods distillers, Popcorn was an icon and became famous for promoting his illegal trade (even after Hank Williams Jr. helped him sell a legal version). In the latter half of the twentieth century, his sunken eyes, bent-out hat, and long, scraggly gray beard became the imagery of an anachronistic legend. He touted his lifestyle, which is embalmed forever in a History Channel documentary. Every waking moment of Popcorn's life was dedicated to making moonshine. After he was eventually arrested in 1999, he committed suicide to avoid serving a year and a half in prison. Cue the banjo.

PREMATURE WHISKEY

Hootenanny aside, white dog is essentially the precursor to all of the finest whiskies in the world. Like a *blanco* tequila or a white rum, it's just whiskey in its white, unaged form. Until recently, you could only try decent white whiskey behind closed doors or on distillery tours. Scotland would gag at the thought, and it's illegal to sell white whiskey in Canada. But in the United States, it's mostly fair game. I was handed a ladle of clear unaged MAKER'S MARK bourbon right off of the still in Loretto, Kentucky. It had a delicious warm and fresh, sweet corn taste and was so smooth that I didn't realize that I had just gulped down 130 proof white dog. Although you can buy a bottle of MAKER'S MARK unaged whiskey at the distillery (it's watered down to 90 proof), the company has decided against selling it elsewhere. It's seen as an unfinished product on its way to becoming world-famous bourbon. Likewise, you would never go to a fancy French *boulangerie* and buy a bag of dough. The Crystal Pepsi (clear cola) of the early 1990s was novel, but it too seemed incomplete. The clear white whiskey is only one step in the process, and many distillers don't want to part with hundreds of years of whiskey history, even if you do love drinking it.

Luckily, even though the vast majority of distilleries don't bottle their whiskey until it is aged, others see huge potential for the spirit with a new generation of drinkers. The simple fact that it's easier, faster, and cheaper to produce an unaged product has helped fuel a trend in the United States. Many new American distilleries are launching with a white whiskey to quench thirst and start selling their wares while they wait for their whiskies to ripen. Although you probably have not heard of most of them, they are worth seeking out. **DEATH'S DOOR** distillery is making a wheated white whiskey, and the famous **BUFFALO TRACE** distillery has released three different white whiskies, each made with a different mixture of grains. These white whiskies lack the deep, round caramel flavor of their bourbon counterparts, but drinking them side by side allows you to pick out some of the grain flavors that are usually covered up by years in oak. They are great to throw into cocktails as a tasty replacement for vodka, or to lighten up drinks that would usually be made with aged whiskey.

WHITE LIES

The naming of white dog is a ridiculous marathon of hurdles that falls into the labyrinth of regulations surrounding the marketing of alcohol. As the rule book goes, to be a white "whiskey," the liquid has to touch some sort of oak barrel, if ever so briefly. Many companies that are now selling white whiskey run the liquid through wooden pipes or let it rest in a barrel for part of an afternoon. On the bottle of **FINGER LAKES DISTILLING**'s white whiskey, **WHITE PIKE**, it's clearly noted that the whiskey has aged for a full eighteen minutes in a bourbon barrel. It's a technicality: aging for eighteen minutes, or even seventy-two hours in the case of **DEATH'S DOOR**, most definitely doesn't add, subtract, or multiply anything to the flavor. Without brands going through the step of touching the spirit to oak, the government regulatory boards would clamp down: the alcohol wouldn't be whiskey, there's no "moonshine" category, and it sure isn't vodka. Even though calling white dog "moonshine" connotes that it was made illegally, a few companies have actually reclaimed the term to bring back the mystery and lore to their alcohol. Today, you can actually buy legal so-called moonshine, marketed by companies riding on the coattails of romanticized bootleggers and Southern rebels. **GEORGIA MOON** goes the distance and even sells its corn whiskey in scantily labeled Mason jars for effect.

White dog doesn't sit on the same barstool as good ol' American bourbons or ryes and shouldn't be compared to any batch of Scotch—it's like apples and, well, apple pie. Although Japanese and Scottish distillers would never even consider bottling white whiskey, and **BUSHMILLS**'s employees would never pour themselves some of their "baby Bushmills," a couple of other Irish distilleries are producing *poitín*, Europe's version of moonshine. However you end up getting your hands on a glass, it is a fun way to learn more about whiskey and a tasty alternative to other white spirits. It's a great exercise to find a white whiskey and an aged whiskey from the same producer to taste your way through the years. Since white whiskey is a new product behind the modern bar, bartenders are getting creative with it. No one is here to tell you that there's only one way to drink it. The trend surged in the 2000s, in part due to a craze for throwback cocktails, renewed interest in Prohibition-style drinks, and an onslaught of new distilleries eager to kick up their cash flow.

INTO YOUR MOUTH

A bartender once told me that white whiskey is like a distiller wearing only his underwear. That doesn't paint a pretty picture, but it's a clear analogy. White dog is a spirit with a very clean taste of its grains and a portal into the craft of the distiller. If it's made from corn, you can actually taste the corn—and many white whiskies have a sweet white cornbread flavor. If it's rye, you'll taste the spicy, drier notes (think rye bread; it's the same grain), and barley will give it a rounder, malty flavor. And yes, Whoppers candies and malt ball chocolates have some of that very same malted barley in them. Wheat-based white dog tends to have a subtle sweetness, and an oat-based spirit will remind you a bit of—you guessed it—oatmeal. It's a fantastic diving board from which to leap straight into understanding whiskies and whiskey aging. Before you break open a bottle of MACALLAN 12 or a BAKER'S bourbon that has been aging for seven years, try tasting a newborn.

Since white dog doesn't get to mellow in a barrel, it lacks the vanilla, oak, and wood flavors that are so prevalent in aged whiskies. If your friends don't like whiskey, they'll be shocked when you pour them a "prewhiskey." Also, be forewarned: white dog can have a harsh burn; in other words, you'll immediately notice the alcohol in it. When it is first made, it can come out at super-high proof, and although whiskey can lose some of its burn when it is hanging out in a barrel, white dog doesn't have that advantage. Most brands will cut it with water to make it palatable. If you've got a bottle that is too strong for your liking, try it over some ice or with a splash of water. It's young and wild, but it is a fun spirit to shake up with your drinks.

If you're making cocktails and you're working with a good-quality white dog (meaning that you enjoy the taste), let the spirit shine. It will work best in drinks that don't overpower the subtle flavors of the grain. Each brand can be made from one or more different grains, and it is a great start to taste your bottle neat—perhaps even straight out of the bottle for maximum effect—then decide where to go from there. Since white dog isn't aged, it's a cheap product to make and easy on the pocketbook. Chances are your local liquor store will sell one or two labels, but keep checking in, as many of the new brands are making their way across the country into your town.

SPEAKEASY

This is as authentic as it gets.

4 oz/120 ml unaged whiskey, at room temperature

Pour whiskey into a glass. Down it before the feds show up.

UPPER EAST SIDE

Jessica Maria, San Francisco

Here's a take on the Manhattan—except that it's white and uses an expensive craft brand, hence the name.

1½ oz /45 ml Hudson New York Corn Whiskey or other white whiskey
¾ oz/25 ml Dolin Blanc or other sweet vermouth
3 dashes of Regans' Orange Bitters No. 6
Ice cubes
1 brandied cherry, for garnish

Combine the whiskey, vermouth, and bitters in a mixing glass with ice cubes and stir until well chilled, 20 to 30 seconds. Strain into a coupe glass and garnish with the cherry before serving.

FINAL WHISPER

Peter Vestinos, Chicago

Peter Vestinos is a bartender who has helped shape cocktail menus across the United States. This drink is a play on the classic cocktail known as the Last Word. Peter recommends that people take old recipes that they know and swap out ingredients. Here, the yellow Chartreuse is a substitute for green, and the white whiskey replaces the traditional gin. This cocktail is simple, supertasty, and allows the white whiskey to shine.

1 oz/30 ml Death's Door or other white whiskey
¾ oz/25 ml yellow Chartreuse
¾ oz/25 ml maraschino liqueur
1 oz/30 ml fresh lemon juice
Ice cubes
1 thyme sprig, for garnish

Combine the whiskey, Chartreuse, maraschino liqueur, and lemon juice in a cocktail shaker with ice cubes and shake vigorously until well chilled, 20 to 30 seconds. Strain into a chilled martini glass and lay the thyme sprig across the rim before serving.

AMERICA
THE
BEAUTIFUL

XXX

At its birth, the United States of America was suckling on a bottle of whiskey. In colonial America, the picture of a man sitting on his porch in the shade of a willow tree and chewing on a piece of wheat would be incomplete if a glass of whiskey wasn't painted into the scene. Nowadays, grabbing a round of whiskey sours while dancing to a "Billie Jean" remix at a forty-eighth-floor rooftop club in Midtown Manhattan might not feel superpatriotic, but it's continuing a tradition established by the likes of George Washington, Thomas Jefferson, and a long lineage of American distillers. Whiskey was not invented in the Home of the Brave, but like beer, burritos, and Chinese food, it was Americanized here.

Many Irish and Scottish immigrants brought with them the knowledge of whiskey making and an unquenchable thirst to get liquored. Luckily, they left the kilts behind. It's an interesting history lesson mixed with revolutionaries, visionaries, and hillbillies; it's a story fraught with violence and a mobster underworld during Prohibition. In the end, the United States redefined a European invention, creating a truly American product that is perhaps one of the last great American exports, along with baseball and Coca-Cola.

The first American whiskies were made around the Pennsylvania area and used rye, a crop that grew well in the colonies and made both a tasty spirit and the bread for a hearty pastrami sandwich. But in reality, the United States has an obsession with corn, and her vast Midwestern grain fields have fueled one of the biggest booze industries in the world. Today, corn is grown on nearly half a million U.S. farms, making it one of the most widely grown cereal grains in North America. The surplus from bumper crops was readily turned into corn whiskey—liquid gold. To this day, the federal government subsidizes the corn industry every year with billions of dollars to influence farmers to produce obscene amounts of the grain. It makes its way into syrups for sodas, starch for cakes, biodiesel for energy, and oil for fries, and it gets fermented and distilled for bourbon's sake. It's not the grain at the base of *every* American whiskey, but it set the stage for bourbon's production and helped establish a unique spirit.

The alcohol industry boomed along with the country and, soon enough, the government set out to create a unique product to call its own. Although any whiskey made within its borders is officially an American whiskey, the country wanted a liquor that screamed U-S-A like a rowdy fan at a baseball game. The French have Champagne, which can only be made in a particular region of France, the Portuguese have port, and the Americans would have bourbon that would be known worldwide but made only Stateside.

THE BIG BOURBON

Learning a few categories of American whiskey will give you points on a compass to help navigate your tongue and understand what direction you're headed. Although rye and Tennessee whiskey are also popular, bourbon has got the name, it's got the fame, and it is perhaps the most commonly confused spirit in the country. Bourbon is any whiskey made in the United States from at least 51 percent corn and aged in charred new oak barrels. There are a few other specifications about how strong it can be and some technical production regulations, but we can leave those to the distillers. Oddly, the rules for marketing a whiskey as bourbon don't apply everywhere in the world. If you're sitting on a beach in Mexico and you're confused, grab a margarita.

Laws and More Laws

While the history of whiskey in the United States is a story of chance and happenstance, the legal structure of American bourbon is highly intentional. The federal government spelled out specific laws to establish strict guidelines for the spirit. Bourbon rules were started by protocols established under President Theodore Roosevelt in 1906, modified by President Taft in 1909, and amended throughout the twentieth century. The government has carved out nearly every detail of the liquid's production and it continues to be one of the most regulated spirits in the world. Bourbon grew and developed through the Great Depression, Prohibition, two world wars, and the recession of the 2000s. Although many new styles of American whiskey are now on the market, bourbon still walks in the footprints of your great-grandfather when he was hitting the bars.

Farmers and lobbyists helped shape bourbon laws to ensure their own success. The lumber industry and coopers (barrel-makers) were clever, as well: they influenced government regulations in 1938 to ensure that only new American wooden barrels could be used in bourbon making. This drove up the cost of making the spirit and guaranteed that distillers would keep coopers in business. It helped to maintain a level of consistency in bourbon and provided an endless supply of used barrels that eventually go to Scotland for aging Scotch, are fashioned into vessels for aging Tabasco sauce, or are turned into giant flowerpots for customers at Wal-Mart.

Corn farmers, who pushed to have our native spirit made with huge quantities of their crop, were the other major influence on bourbon regulations. The influence of both the farming and lumber industries on federal regulations kept jobs in the United

States and had a large impact on the taste of your alcohol. **To this day, when you drink bourbon, you're supporting the United States economy in a big way.**

All bourbons are equal but some are more equal than others. If a whiskey is bourbon, the bottle will say so. If you pick up a bottle and it says anything else, don't be fooled. It may taste great, but it's not classic American bourbon. Wearing a bourbon name tag is sexy, but it's by no means a marker of supreme quality, and there are several things that distillers can do to change up the way their bourbon tastes. In fact, even within the range of available bourbons, the cost and flavor spread is a broad one. A bottle can range from the cost of your lunch to sixty times that much for a rare label. Ask for a whiskey sour at your local bar and you're more than likely to get the cheaper stuff.

What Else Is in It?

Although bourbon must contain at least 51 percent corn, a variety of other grains can make up the rest of the spirit. Like all American whiskies, bourbon can include rye, wheat, or barley—or even oats, spelt, or other grains—and the choice of ingredients can alter the flavor significantly. Unfortunately for consumers, the secondary grains in bourbons are usually not called out on the bottles, but most of the information is readily available online. As a general rule, more rye will make your bourbon spicy, like the kick in rye bread. BASIL HAYDEN'S is made with a lot of rye and so are the bourbons of BUFFALO TRACE, WOODFORD RESERVE, BULLEIT, and OLD GRAND-DAD. Wheat will bring a soft, sweet, smooth taste to any whiskey; think of the sweetness in fresh whole-wheat bread. The best-known wheated bourbon is MAKER'S MARK, but several others are out there, including OLD FITZGERALD, OLD WELLER, and the elusive **PAPPY VAN WINKLE**. When corn becomes the minority ingredient, a whiskey gives up its bourbon title, but it can still be a delicious American whiskey. If you don't know where to start, figure out what flavors strike your fancy and head in that direction.

The second thing that distillers change up to give each whiskey a unique taste is the yeast strain. Like a sourdough starter, each yeast strain has been passed down for generations and has its own distinctive style. Unless you're a chemist, talking about yeast strains is worse than counting sheep. And since yeast strains are highly proprietary and are almost always patented, if anyone told you, they'd have to kill you. **FOUR ROSES** is a notable exception to the penchant for secrecy, and the folks at the brand are excited to explain the effects of using their five different strains. Rumor has it that **JIM BEAM**'s distiller takes a jar of his yeast home every weekend—just in case. But since brands don't say what yeast they use, you can't choose a whiskey based on the genetic makeup of its yeast anyhow.

Aging

The manner in which a whiskey is aged also greatly affects the spirit. As explained in the chapter on white dog, freshly made alcohol is not whiskey until it touches oak, which means new whiskey can't be bourbon yet, either. It's the new oak barrels that are burnt (charred) on the inside that give bourbon its famous warm, oaky, caramel taste. Spraying fire inside a barrel to scorch it isn't just a pyromaniac's ritual. It's the step that pulls out the vanilla and sugar flavors and also caramelizes the wood, which is what gives whiskey its traditional golden color. The barrel becomes an inside-out tea bag: the longer the whiskey steeps, the more flavor it draws from the wood.

Most likely, the first whiskey makers to burn the inside of the barrel were repurposing casks that had previously held fish or sauerkraut. Although golden bourbon wasn't the intended outcome, neither was anchovy whiskey. Another legend gives credit to Baptist preacher Elijah Craig for accidentally burning the first barrel (and realizing it did wonders for his whiskey).

Most barrels used in bourbon making are nearly identical. They may have a little more or a little less burnt wood, but the wood is all from white oak trees grown in the United States. The most prominent differences among bourbons come from the amount of time that they hang out in the barrel and where exactly that barrel ages. In southern bourbon territory, distilleries make a big deal about the big multistory, prisonlike structures where the whiskey sleeps for years. While the summers are hot as hell, the winters get nippy and the changes in temperature cause more flavor from the wood to seep into the alcohol. The temperature differences are magnified by each barrel's location in the warehouse. Like an attic, the warehouses collect heat, and in the middle of a 104°F/40°C summer, the top levels can be 20°F/11°C hotter than the bottom rows. The air in these buildings has an incredible aroma and is saturated with alcohol that evaporates as the whiskey ages. This evaporating mix of water and alcohol is called the angel's share. Keep your mouth open when touring the space. You might be able to inhale enough whiskey to make your trip worth it, or capture a couple of drops leaking from a barrel.

For the majority of American whiskies, the final flavor comes from a mix of barrels from all parts of the warehouse. Master blenders scout out the prime spots and the barrels that should be mixed together for each brand's style or flavor. Barrels from the warehouse's sweet spots are chosen for the small-batch bourbons and the single-barrel bottles. For example, the small-batch brand

BOOKER'S always draws from barrels on the fifth and sixth levels of the warehouse because the temperatures are just right. Single-barrel bottlings are also chosen from the best areas of the warehouse. Inspired by Colonel Blanton (the other Kentucky colonel), who was one of the foremen at what is now the **BUFFALO TRACE** distillery, **BLANTON'S** launched in 1984 as the first mainstream single-barrel bourbon. Small-batch and single-barrel whiskies are the alcohol industry's answer to the food revolution and trends in gourmet imbibing. Almost all large brands now have some sort of premium product. Turn to these for a sipping whiskey. If you're a millionaire, no one will stop you from making these your well whiskies for cocktails.

In general, the older a bourbon, the darker it will be. The strict laws governing bourbon dictate that no coloring can be added, which means that every pixel of color comes from the inside of the barrel. One of the hardest facts to swallow is that age isn't a marker of quality. In fact, too much time spent in a barrel can sometimes turn whiskey into alcoholic sawdust. Any tea connoisseur can recite the exact amount of time a particular tea should steep. Similarly, a key to making the perfect whiskey is bottling the barrel at the right moment.

In the end, it's all about preference. If you like sucking on lumber, look for old whiskies. On warm summer evenings, I'd go after younger, lighter bourbons. If a bottle has an age on it, that is the youngest whiskey that can be in the bottle. There is no perfect age for bourbon. The minimum for straight bourbon is two years, but many of the big brands stay put for four to six years. If you're hoping to unload some cash, you can find bourbon around the twenty-year mark. Instead of marking bottles with the number of times the earth has gone around the sun, some distilleries describe their whiskies with names, numbers, or colors. A handful of brands, including MAKER'S MARK and BULLEIT, don't say how old the bourbon is on the bottle, mostly because it allows them flexibility, and like a thirty-year-old man who acts like he's eighteen, sometimes maturity is more important than age.

Many of these nuanced techniques and choices are common not only in bourbon making but for most American whiskies.

Ground Zero

The namesake of bourbon is Bourbon County, Kentucky, by all accounts the metaphysical center of the bourbon world even though no bourbon is actually made within the county limits. In fact, bourbon can be made anywhere on American soil; a bourbon made in Honolulu would have the same seal of approval as one made in Bardstown, Kentucky. Legend has it that the name *bourbon* stuck because Americans were brownnosing the French (to whom they were shipping loads of whiskey in French-owned New Orleans). Bourbon, named after a gallant ruling family in France, was a word that the French could pronounce with a certain *je ne sais quoi*. As a form of gratitude to France's aid in the Revolutionary War and because of their colonial proximity to the early United States, enclaves of the American South have complex ties to the French. Bourbon County is hardly the only area whose name was borrowed from *la République française*. The cities of Versailles (pronounced with a Southern accent, Versales) and Paris are nestled in the Kentucky countryside not far from Louisville.

Bourbon is now being produced across the United States, but Kentucky remains the symbolic and physical heart of bourbon making. More than 80 percent of U.S. bourbon comes from Kentucky, and it is where the culture continues to flourish. There are more barrels of bourbon sitting around Kentucky right now than there are people in the state. Abraham Lincoln, who was born in Kentucky and saw it as a key region in the Union's fight against the Confederacy, once famously said of the state, "I hope to have God on my side, but I must have Kentucky." Its beautiful rolling hills, ancient oaks, and white picket fences are carbon copies of my Civil War daydreams during American history class. Although I wasn't old enough to fit bourbon into my report about General Robert E. Lee, it was just as much a part of the battle as bayonets and blood. Lincoln knew whiskey was important to keep his troops' morale afloat and condoned General Ulysses S. Grant's drinking habits, even inquiring as to what brand Grant drank so that he might give bottles to the rest of his generals. Working on managing your own troops? Grant is said to have loved OLD CROW bourbon, a brand you can still find at the back of the bottom shelf in liquor stores everywhere.

Kentucky's bourbon regions are in the absolute middle of nowhere. Aside from world-famous horses and delicious bourbon (which many locals will tell you are both the result of the wonderful limestone-filtered water), you'll find an occasional McDonald's and a whole lot of churches. Although at one time it was home to hundreds of small-farm distilleries, Kentucky was also one of the hotbeds of the temperance movement. Even though booze has been legal in the United States since 1933, much of America is still living under prohibition. To this day, around 80 of the 120 counties in Kentucky are dry or moist. (The term *moist* describes a county that falls somewhere between wet, which allows the sale of alcohol in liquor stores and bars, and dry, which prohibits the sale of alcohol everywhere. Many dry counties are moving in this direction to sell booze in restaurants and other venues to take advantage of tax opportunities, though residents still won't be able to head down to the corner shop for a bottle.) The other 40 wet counties in the state have the most amazing drive-through liquor stores I've ever seen.

Historic bourbon territory is relatively small, with its farmhouse-dotted fields stretching only a couple of hours from end to end. It's a juxtaposition of idyllic pastures and white-bread middle-American suburbia. Bourbon still fits well into Southern culture as a panache of small-town porch life. As noted earlier, the first whiskies in the Americas were made around Pennsylvania, but the practice started to move south when the government began giving four-hundred-acre land grants to settlers to grow corn. The strategy behind the giveaway was to expand west, have a food safety net based on a multipurpose grain, and put a layer of settlers between the government and any hostile neighbors. If you recall anything from your high-school history class, the Whiskey Rebellion is lodged somewhere in your brain between the (first) Tea Party and the Emancipation Proclamation. The rebellion was made up of settlers on the frontier protesting a new tax on whiskey. Since the Northeasterners drank more wine and cider and made far less whiskey, Westerners felt that the tax fell on them unfairly. This was, of course, a generation that had fled from the unfair taxes of the British and was still allergic to big government. The rebels were quelled by the military in 1794, and soon after, many moved south to flee oppressive government regulation. It wasn't until Thomas Jefferson repealed the tax and then authorized the Louisiana Purchase in 1803 that whiskey started to spread faster than smallpox. With a new frontier, distillers and farmers had more land and easy access to the Mississippi River, a water route that allowed them to trade their spirits with the rest of the world.

Some of the most famous bourbon brands got their start just about the same time the government was buying land from Napoléon. **BUFFALO TRACE**'s oldest building dates back to 1792 and still sits on the lush banks where buffalo used to cross the Kentucky River on their seasonal migrations. Evan Williams was setting up his distillery in 1783, and the **JIM BEAM** brand has had family members involved in whiskey for seven generations, led by Mr. Jacob Beam. Bourbon is the drink of American history.

Kentucky continues to embrace bourbon's Southern roots and is promoting bourbon as a historical cornerstone of the South. To promote whiskey tourism, the city of Louisville has even set up an urban bourbon trail through Louisville bars. At your sweaty fingertips you have all the best bourbon and most authentically American cocktails in the world. Although Kentucky senator Henry Clay popularized the mint julep before Prohibition, the refreshing drink in the iconic frosted silver cup is still revered in the South with iconic gusto. Since 1938, the mint julep has been the official drink of the Kentucky Derby, with more than one hundred thousand sold at Churchill Downs every year. If your bet has paid out, you can also try a premium $1,000 mint julep made with the official bourbon, **WOODFORD RESERVE**, mint grown in California, and ice imported from France, all served in a hand-engraved julep cup. It's an absurd, over-the-top drink, but the money all goes to charity.

Unlike wineries that might produce only expensive high-end bottles, most distilleries turn out a range of whiskies to satisfy an array of consumers and paychecks. **BUFFALO TRACE** makes bottom-shelf blends like **ANCIENT AGE** that you're likely to find collecting dust at the corner store, but they also make some of the most expensive bourbons money can buy, including **PAPPY VAN WINKLE**, the extremely rare and old bottles that are auctioned online for the price of a flat-screen TV (even liquor stores in towns near the distillery get only one or two bottles a year). Although the same equipment is used for the whiskies, differences come from the specific percentages of grain, where the barrels age in the warehouse, and which barrels are chosen for a bottling.

There are fewer than a dozen whiskey distilleries in the South, with the majority of Kentucky bourbons coming from only six of them. Although sipping on a **MAKER'S MARK** in a hotel in Singapore might lead you to think that the alcohol is made in a giant factory, in reality, most bourbon distilleries (including **MAKER'S MARK**) are family heirlooms and retain the personal charm you might expect from a local diner. Brands are often named after familial legends or are nods to iconic bourbon pioneers and are often woven with stories on the bottles.

JIM BEAM, for example, has the name of the family all over it. Although the business was actually started by Jacob Beam in 1795, Jim took over four generations later and helped to continue the line that is now headed up by the seventh generation. The brand also has a small-batch bourbon, **BOOKER'S**, which was named for Jim's grandson. On the bottle of **JIM BEAM WHITE LABEL**, you can trace the ancestry of the brand. Jim Beam's cousin was the first master distiller at **HEAVEN HILL**, a large family-run distillery that makes **ELIJAH CRAIG** and **EVAN WILLIAMS**. It's a company that still has a Beam family member as its master distiller. Bourbon is a wonderfully small and incestuous world.

Established in 1888, the **FOUR ROSES** brand moved into its current distillery in 1910. The building, done in colonial Spanish style, is the center of bourbon land. The brand's namesake is a family story unto itself. After courting a woman for ages, Paul Jones Jr., the founder of **FOUR ROSES**, invited her to a dance and told her to wear a corsage of four roses if she accepted his marriage proposal. She showed up with massive roses around her wrist and the rest is history. Coincidentally, since 1904, the rose has been the official flower of the Kentucky Derby: the winner is draped with a blanket of red roses. The **FOUR ROSES** brand has been iconic throughout American history: it sits on the top of Times Square in Alfred Eisenstaedt's famous photograph of a VJ Day soldier taking a woman into his arms on the street. It was also one of the big brands that produced cheap and massive quantities of alcohol post-Prohibition. Although **FOUR ROSES** stopped sales domestically in the 1950s to focus on international distribution (it's still big in Asia), the brand picked itself up in the United States in 1996 and is growing strong with a higher focus on smaller-batch quality.

Howdy Neighbor!

Another denomination of American whiskey that often gets confused with bourbon is its neighbor to the south, Tennessee whiskey. Around the same time that many of the bourbon giants were born in Kentucky, a five-foot-two gentleman with a colossal mustache set up shop. With a name that would later grace billboards around the world, Jack Daniel and his contemporary, a fellow named George Dickel, were part of a growing trend of whiskey makers in Tennessee. Somewhere along the line, both Daniel and Dickel picked up the custom of filtering their whiskey over charcoal to make a smoother spirit. Both distilleries continue the practice, and it is the primary difference that sets them apart from their bourbon counterparts. Both distilleries burn large bonfires of sugar-maple wood and filter their unaged whiskies over the chunks of burnt charcoal—in Jack's case, one drop at a time. It's an arduous process that makes the spirit lighter and smoother and filters out some of the impurities. **JACK DANIEL'S** premium label, **GENTLEMAN JACK**, takes that same process and does it twice. The rest of the Tennessee whiskey-making process is pretty much identical to bourbon making. Like Kentucky, Tennessee has a mishmash of dry, wet, and moist counties. Both distilleries happen to be based in dry areas, although JACK DANIEL'S bends the rules a bit to give a bottle to each employee on the first Friday of each month.

JACK DANIEL'S has grown into one of the top-selling whiskies in the world. Its iconic square bottle and black label (launched by Jack's nephew to commemorate his death) can be seen from across the bar. It's a brand that is shrouded in legends and history and a swirling marketing campaign that has captured the attention of generations of consumers. Although the brand tends to show up in chaotic party scenes, like John Belushi downing a bottle in *Animal House*, it was also the brand of choice for Frank Sinatra. It's among the few select brands that have weaseled their way into the name of world-famous bar drinks. Jack and Coke, anyone? It was a Jack and Coke that was my own first foray into whiskey. Jack has been around since the mid-1800s, with a hiatus during Prohibition, and is one of the most recognized alcohol brands in more than 135 countries around the world. The *No. 7* on the front label means absolutely nothing—or at least no one actually knows. Perhaps it was Jack's final test batch of whiskey, how many girlfriends he swooned over, or his lucky number. The grandson of Welsh immigrants didn't have all the luck of the Irish, however. Jack kicked his safe after forgetting the combination and cut his toe. The cut became infected and led to gangrene, which ended up killing the whiskey tycoon. Of course, he could have survived if he just soaked his toe in some of his own fresh whiskey, which is strong enough to be a powerful antiseptic.

Started around the same time as **JACK DANIEL'S**, **GEORGE DICKEL** was also shut down during Prohibition. After a few failed attempts at producing the whiskey in other states, many years passed before the distillery was able to begin operating again. It now sits in Cascade Hollow, a picturesque valley that must have inspired decades of colonial painters. There is little in the area to distract the staff from making whiskey, and **DICKEL** is among the few distilleries that still make the stuff in an old-school style. Manual scales and traditional equipment keep the small-town charm of the brand. Half of the world has never heard of **DICKEL**, and the other half can't stop talking about it. I've met folks who only drink **DICKEL** and folks who have bottles tattooed across their biceps. A few years back, a couple of die-hard fans built and drove a replica of a 1910 whiskey delivery truck across the country from California to Cascade Hollow just to show their love for the brand. The truck was donated to the distillery and still sits in the front room at the facility. Tennesseans must love numbers: to go along with Jack's numerical nomenclature, **DICKEL** makes a No. 8 and a No. 12 and again, no one knows the significance. The brand also makes an award-winning **CASCADE HOLLOW** whiskey and a small-batch **BARREL SELECT**.

GOOD OL' BOYS DRINKING WHISKEY AND RYE

Rye whiskey in America predates the founding of our country. It was the grain that grew best around the original colonies and the Northeast. When Irish and Scottish immigrants made the journey across the Atlantic, they were ready to make whiskey with whatever they could find; rye was cheap and Irish immigrants knew how to use it. George Washington even made rye whiskey at Mount Vernon. It's more American than Mickey Mouse.

Basically, the only thing that makes rye whiskey different from bourbon is that it has a majority of rye instead of corn. While many bourbons are made with a bit of rye in them, on a spectrum, a bourbon becomes a rye whiskey when the rye grains tip over that magic 51 percent. Rye grain makes whiskey spicier and drier, and you'll often be able to taste more of the grain in the flavor. It hits on the back of your tongue. **BULLEIT** bourbon, for example, has a lot of rye in it, so it's going to be relatively spicy and much closer to rye whiskey than its counterparts. **BULLEIT** rye (with the green label) is even spicier. Similarly, **OLD GRAND-DAD** bourbon has a lot of rye in its recipe, but less so than **(rī)**[1]—pronounced "rye one"—a premium rye made by the same company. Rye is commonly made by distilleries that make bourbons, so many of the processes are the same. **By now it should be clear that the words to Don McLean's "American Pie" are redundant: rye *is* whiskey.**

Rye whiskies all but died when Prohibition halted the alcoholic beverage industry in the States. Instead, rye was used to add flavor to light Canadian blends, and to this day, rye is synonymous with whiskey up north. Even after Prohibition, rye took a great deal longer to catch up for lost time. Since it's spicier, drier, and more bitter than bourbon, it wasn't exactly in line with the American palate trashed by Prohibition potables. As a raw ingredient, rye is less common and less subsidized (and therefore more expensive) than corn. The buried treasure is only recently being uncovered; it's nothing new, but we're seeing it coming back in its own mini-revolution.

Fueled by a growing desire for leaner, spicier liquor and a fanaticism for pre-Prohibition drinks, rye is moving up to the front of the bar. It's finding its way back into classic cocktails on menus and is a prime ingredient for bartenders shaping their own creations. The trend started its engines in the 1990s when Fritz

Maytag, then owner of San Francisco's Anchor Steam Brewery, decided to get into distilling. With a knack for classic recipes and a passion for the old-school way of doing things, he started making rye whiskey in the traditional American style. Just like the Anchor Steam beer that Maytag also championed, his **OLD POTRERO** rye is a throwback to the days when California gold miners were slinging cocktails and prostitutes across the bar. Today, rye is made across the country at microdistilleries everywhere from California and Utah (High West Distillery & Saloon) to a smattering of operations in New York. As tattoo sleeves are replacing tuxedo sleeves, the demand for classic spirits is blossoming. Big bourbon brands have followed suit: **BULLEIT, JIM BEAM, WILD TURKEY, BUFFALO TRACE**, and **HEAVEN HILL** all make rye.

I know a lot of people who aren't keen on bourbon but love a good rye drink. Ryes tend to be more peppery and complex than their sweeter, cornier bourbon counterparts. Those same qualities that kept them off the shelves after Prohibition are now bringing them back into the American liquor cabinet. For beer drinkers, rye is to pale ale what bourbon is to amber ale. The amber is sweeter and fuller but often less complex. Cheaper rye brands like **OLD OVERHOLT, RITTENHOUSE**, and **JIM BEAM** are fantastic and perfectly priced for cocktails like the famed Sazerac, while small-batch and higher-end rye is great on its own. Substitute rye for bourbon in your other drinks for a drier, spicier cocktail.

DRINK A BOTTLE BY ITS COVER

Directed by government regulations and antiquated laws passed years ago, whiskey makers put all sorts of titles and tags on their bottles. Although sometimes the most important details don't make it onto the label, the information that is there hints as to what you're pouring. Headings and descriptions are a peep show into a whiskey's history. There's no need to run off and create flashcards, but knowing a few of the terms will help to make sure you're not just following the North Star for directions.

The first descriptor to keep an eye out for will tell you what grains are in the whiskey. Bourbon? It's mostly corn. Corn whiskey (these aren't common)? It's a whopping 80 percent corn. Rye? It's mostly rye. American single malt? That tells you that the whiskey is made entirely of barley. And 51 percent or more wheat will bestow a wheat whiskey title on a bottle. If a bottle doesn't tell you any of this, it's likely a mix of a bunch of grains.

The word *straight* means that your whiskey isn't mixed with flavorless neutral grain spirits (e.g., vodka) and that it's aged at least two years in a new American oak barrel. It could be straight bourbon, a straight American whiskey, or even a straight rye. Regardless of what it's made from, it's going to be bolder, rounder, and fuller than other blends.

If you see the word *bond* or *bonded* on the bottle, it's got nothing to do with 007. It's an archaic term that has a lot to do with taxes and regulations and tells you that a whiskey was distilled in a single year, at a single distillery, by one distiller. It also means that the whiskey is at least four years old and hits precisely 100 proof. It's like a vintage from a specific winery. Why should you care? It's a clever way to sense the "skill" of the distiller and taste a moment in time.

Unlike a bucket of KFC, if a label on American whiskey says *Kentucky* anywhere, it *really* was made in Kentucky. But Kentucky is just the start; amazing whiskey is flowing across the country. Find out where your whiskey is from. If a bottle says *distilled by*, then you can actually find out where the distillery is (and visit it!). If it says *bottled by*, then a third-party company bottles it. Be cautious of bottles that don't have any information on them. Generic blended whiskies might be cheap, but there might be a good reason why they are keeping secrets. You're not going to learn anything from them no matter how much you drink. But I *have* had some incredible whiskies from unmarked flasks out of a friend's pocket.

PROHIBITION

It's impossible to talk about the development and history of American whiskey without hitting the brick wall that was Prohibition. I've already mentioned it twelve times in this chapter alone. The official prohibition of alcohol in the United States stretched a long fourteen years and had lasting international impacts on the whiskey industry and on trends into the twenty-first century. Tennessee went dry in 1910, and its arduous twenty-three-year booze drought forced hundreds of distilleries to move or close their doors. In a nutshell, Prohibition decimated the American whiskey industry to a stump. Since whiskey ages in a barrel for several years, Prohibition not only poured years of existing whiskey down the sewer pipes but also sent the industry stumbling back a generation and ensured that consumers would have to relearn quality whiskey when it was once again legal. The few distilleries that survived, including what are now **BUFFALO TRACE** and **FOUR ROSES**, were government-approved vendors that legally sold alcohol to fill doctors' prescriptions.

The Eighteenth Amendment shut down the alcohol industry, but it didn't stop people from making, drinking, and selling booze. It moved the scene underground, and making alcohol became a dangerous prospect. It was a cat-and-mouse game, and getting caught could lead to a life spent on Alcatraz. The feds would look for telltale signs of alcohol production: smells, leaks, and shipments leaving under the veil of the shining moon. A little fungus was also a death sentence to bootleggers. As whiskey ages and some of the alcohol evaporates into the air, it feeds the growth of a black fungus on nearby buildings and trees, making for surreal scenery of stark black trees dotted with bright green leaves. It is a common sight up by DICKEL's warehouses and for acres around the JIM BEAM distillery. Although the fungus, *Baudoinia compniacensis*, might be a photographer's dream, it was kryptonite to illicit whiskey makers. Agents would commonly look for black forests to find their prey. In turn, some bootleggers picked up and moved to nearby coal mines where soot covered everything.

Prohibition did more than just strike down the warehouses and stills across the United States. It ripped out the tongue and singed the taste buds of American consumers. A once-lively saloon scene with corseted burlesque dancers, bowler hats, and fanciful cocktails stepped behind false bookshelves and hidden doors. Lighter Canadian whiskies and mass-produced Scotch blends were smuggled in, and drinks lacked the farm-fresh spirits and bold tastes that had dominated the previous 150 years. Getting a good buzz was more important than getting a good drink. The quality of booze plummeted and production came to a standstill. America lost her direction and the country's drinking culture fell years behind the rest of the world.

There You Go Drinking Again

The night Prohibition was repealed must have seen a country partying like it was 1899. Consumers were celebrating drunkenly in the streets, but the American whiskey industry was in shambles. The few distilleries that had operated through Prohibition kicked up production to get the juices flowing. But the majority of distilleries were long gone. Years of moonshine, insipid alcohol, and light blended whiskies led Americans to thirst for drinks that were easy to swill, and vodka flourished in the middle wedge of the century. This was the heyday of illustrated national ad campaigns used to refamiliarize the American public with alcohol. Full-page advertisements sought to reinstate whiskey's place in society as the drink of choice for established white men. Brands fought viciously to recapture consumers and take their slice of the emerging market. Even SMIRNOFF entered the race, marketing itself early as a white whiskey (with no smell and no flavor). FOUR ROSES later launched a campaign that went so far as to freeze long-stemmed red roses in big ice blocks and ship them to liquor stores. The powerhouse of liquor media stopped at no bounds.

The whiskey families who were able to pick up the pieces after Prohibition restarted their stills and reestablished themselves as a new generation of whiskey pioneers. Many entrepreneurs looked to their roots and started up old family traditions. Bill Samuels Sr. was one such forerunner with MAKER'S MARK. A sixth-generation distiller, Bill burned up his family's old recipe after Prohibition and started from scratch to develop an entirely new bourbon. With his wife, Margie, doing the marketing, design, and branding, it was a family affair. Based on Margie's interest in Cognac bottles, she insisted on hand dipping each bottle in red wax to seal it. Why red? Perhaps because Bill and Margie were both graduates of the University of Louisville, where cardinal red rules. Although nowadays the wax is a patented polymer, each bottle is still hand dipped on the factory line at the distillery, and no two look exactly the same. Today, the distillery is under the watch of Rob Samuels, part of the eighth generation to be in the industry.

Prohibition lasted much longer in Tennessee, which completely stunted the growth and development of the state's whiskey industry. JACK DANIEL'S only got up and running after its owner (who happened to be a state senator) helped repeal state prohibition in 1938. The DICKEL distillery took many more years to catch up and didn't start producing whiskey with the original recipe again until the mid-1960s.

Resurrection

Among the new brands hitting the market are a handful of companies that are reaching back a few generations to resurrect old recipes. Perhaps the best known is BULLEIT bourbon. Augustus Bulleit emigrated from France and began making whiskey in Kentucky in the early 1800s. As legend has it, just before the Civil War he inexplicably disappeared on a trip to New Orleans and the brand died out. But his great-great-grandson Tom Bulleit reintroduced it to the country in 1999. A Vietnam veteran and attorney who made big life changes to follow his family heritage, Tom set out to re-create the original recipe. BULLEIT graces bars in dozens of countries, and the tradition continues to be a family affair. Tom touts his bourbon around the country and his daughter, Hollis, is a vocal ambassador and a future face of the brand (as well as part of a new generation of women who are emerging in the industry).

Throughout Prohibition, TEMPLETON rye was made in hidden warehouses and stashed in graves and bales of hay around the Iowa town of the same name. It was known among mobsters for its high quality and, like BULLEIT bourbon, is now back, eighty-five years later and allegedly made according to a Prohibition-era family recipe. MICHTER'S is bringing back the spirit of one of the oldest distilleries in the country. Shut down in 1989, the Pennsylvania distillery is said to have furnished George Washington's troops with rye whiskey during the Revolutionary War. The brand has kicked off once again and is now making a range of whiskies in

Kentucky. In yet another throwback, CYRUS NOBLE was once the whiskey of the gold-seeking miners of California and the bourbon of San Francisco's wild Barbary Coast nightlife. It has been revived by Haas Brothers, the same distilled-spirits merchant that brought it to California in the first place.

Onward Ho!

American whiskies are racing up the curve of the half-pipe. The country is rapidly catching up to where it was before Prohibition, and in some ways, it has already surpassed where it left off. Increased interest in Scotch and single malts has been a catalyst to a growing interest in quality American spirits. The onslaught of new independent distilleries, innovative brands, and big research and development budgets has pushed the boundaries of American whiskey.

Distillers are stepping away from prescribed laws and recommended directions for whiskey making. **It's the generation of trying fresh approaches, and what better way to pave new roads than to make whiskey that knows no boundaries.** JIM BEAM is now making DEVIL'S CUT, a product in which the bourbon that has soaked into the wooden barrels is mixed with standard bourbon. It's big, oaky, and aggressive and another bold innovative move in the industry. Looking to get creative with a new product, MAKER'S MARK launched MAKER'S 46 (its only new product in the last fifty years), in which the company sears several strips of French oak, attaches them to the inside of a traditional American oak bourbon barrel, and then uses the barrel to steep mature bourbon for a few months. The popularity of MAKER'S 46, which is bottled a little stronger than standard MAKER'S MARK, is a testament to the fact that whiskey drinkers are on board with new products.

Even modern food trends have found their way into the bourbon industry. Several established companies have held back from using genetically modified corn but are fairly hush-hush about what goes into their whiskey. They want to keep their options open because the supply of non-GMO corn in the United States is dwindling. Alongside new developments from the classic big companies, we're seeing trends of small organic brands, new recipes, flavored whiskies, and experiments gone right.

CRAFT WHISKEY

The big trend and continued future of American whiskey rests in the craft distilleries and small brands that you've probably never heard of. A spate of microdistillers is growing into a countrywide trend. Recent laws in a couple of states, including New York, have made the barriers to entry much lower for new distilleries, and dozens of independent entrepreneurs are living out their dreams and paving the road with local booze. The number of independent distilleries has more than doubled over the last ten years, and organizations like the American Distilling Institute are fostering the growth of many more.

While dozens of the new distilleries are looking back to traditional pre-Prohibition whiskey and traditional bourbons, many others are throwing spaghetti at the wall to see what sticks. TUTHILLTOWN SPIRITS has made a name for itself in a budding world of innovation. It breaks tradition by using small barrels to speed along the maturing process and is quickly growing a cult following. Like many of the smaller operations, it is assembling a long menu of whiskies, from white dog to "baby bourbon" to an American single malt.

Brands are tossing out tradition and ripping up antiquated recipes to experiment with new flavors. **Distillers are stepping out from customary naming conventions by choosing their own mix of grains, using all sorts of barrels for aging, and testing blends as if their whiskies were watercolors.** HIGH WEST, Utah's only distillery, sells BOURYE, a blend of a rye and a bourbon. It was so popular that a second-generation version, SON OF BOURYE, was introduced. CORSAIR distillery in Nashville, Tennessee, has multiple new styles of whiskies, but none is actually Tennessee whiskey. Several microdistilleries are experimenting with smoking barley with alder and beech wood to change up the flavor of their whiskey; others are roasting and toasting grains to mess with the status quo (and give whiskies more coffee and chocolate characteristics). The old master distiller from MAKER'S MARK is now making bourbon using the *solera* method, an esoteric fractional blending and aging technique traditionally used to make sherry and some rums. Distillers are going back to the drawing table to sketch out new blueprints for the future of American whiskey.

Founded in 1982, California's ST. GEORGE SPIRITS distills anything it can get its hands on. **Aside from distilling crabs, porcini mushrooms, and seaweed, the folks at St. George are western whiskey mavens.** They've been making an American single malt for almost two decades, blending their own bourbon, and are now blazing trends by distilling beer into beer schnapps. This is undoubtedly one of the big trends looming in test labs. CHARBAY in Northern California is making whiskies from IPAs and pilsners. STRANAHAN'S distillery in Colorado partners with a local brewery to make beer for its whiskey, and ROGUE BREWERY in Oregon has come out with a whiskey from its own ales. **Enjoy smoked stouts, golden ambers, or**

hoppy imperial IPAs? Why not distill them in the name of whiskey. With microdistilleries popping up in towns everywhere, it's getting much easier. Many brewers are going to become distillers.

I could write volumes on the emerging trends, and indeed, a lot of people are trying to follow the snowballing industry. The American craft segment of whiskey isn't just growing laterally. Some of these brands are slowly making their way out of their little towns and neighborhood distilleries and into specialized liquor shops everywhere. This is just the beginning.

FLAVOR FLAV

A friend once asked me why bourbon distillers keep within legal guidelines for the sake of writing bourbon on their bottles. If there were a market for it, why wouldn't a distiller create the tastiest drink he or she could, regardless of what it's called? Welcome to the world of flavored whiskies. These aren't bourbons, they aren't ryes, and technically speaking, they aren't whiskies at all. Several larger brands are testing out small armies of flavors. Using mostly naturally occurring tastes, they are a far cry from trends of bubble-gum and whipped-cream vodka. JIM BEAM now makes an entire line of RED STAG, bottles of spiced, black-cherry, and honey-tea whiskey. JACK DANIEL'S, WILD TURKEY, and EVAN WILLIAMS all make honey whiskey, and MAKER'S MARK even produces a mint julep flavor, though it's not easy to find outside of Kentucky. LEOPOLD BROTHERS, a microdistillery in Denver, is making flavored whiskies with apples, blackberries, and even two different kinds of peaches. While I'm still waiting for an umami-laden foie gras whiskey to come out, the other flavors are a great way to ease your friends into the basic whiskey taste. Of course, if you know what you're doing, you can always infuse your own (it's not that difficult).

American whiskey is about as patriotic as many people get. Bourbon is my Fourth of July drink, and rye seems to make its way into too many of my cocktails. The United States is producing whiskies that insult the Scots, anger the Japanese, and make the Irish jealous. While the rest of the world watches, homegrown distillers are winning the hearts and the livers of our generation. There's good sense to it all: the country was literally and politically founded on the fact that American whiskey is a beautiful thing and worth making, or at least drinking if you don't own a still. Believe me, our amber waves of grain weren't all turned into bread.

MINT JULEP

Fun fact: The word *julep* comes from the Persian word *julab*, or "rose water." It has the same root as *gulab jamun*, the popular Indian dessert of milk-rich dough balls soaked in a rose-water syrup.

5 fresh mint sprigs
1 tsp sugar
2½ oz/75 ml Woodford Reserve Bourbon
Crushed ice

Muddle 3 of the mint sprigs, the sugar, and a splash of the bourbon in the bottom of a silver cup. Add some crushed ice and the rest of the bourbon and stir until frost starts to form on the outside of the cup. Top off with more ice and the remaining mint sprigs before serving. Pretend that you know a lot about horseracing.

OLD FASHIONED

Thought to be made of the most basic ingredients a cocktail can contain, the old fashioned is a solid go-to drink when done properly. First served at a gentlemen's club in Louisville, Kentucky, in 1880, it was bastardized throughout the latter half of the twentieth century with chunks of fruit and maraschino cherries. Perhaps through osmosis of cocktail scenes in *Mad Men*, it's now popping up in well-known cocktail bars, where it is being re-created in pre-Prohibition style, as well as with new twists.

1 brown-sugar cube
3 dashes of Angostura bitters
2 oz/60 ml Maker's Mark bourbon, or rye for a drier cocktail
Ice cubes
1 orange peel strip, for garnish

Place the sugar cube at the bottom of a rocks glass, top with the bitters, and muddle together. Pour in the bourbon, add ice, and stir well. Twist the orange peel over the glass to release its oils and then drop it into the drink before serving.

SAZERAC

The Sazerac is America's first cocktail, and if ordered at a bar, it's served with an air of cocktail expertise. Invented by Antoine Amédée Peychaud, a Creole apothecary who moved to New Orleans from Saint-Domingue (today's Haiti) in the late eighteenth century, the Sazerac still uses Peychaud's brand bitters. Named for the brand of Cognac that it was first made with, the Sazerac later changed to be made with American rye whiskey (when France's Cognac industry was decimated by a plague of bugs). It's pure booze, but an incredibly perfected mix of flavors. The Sazerac became the official drink of New Orleans in 2008 and remains one of my staples.

Splash of absinthe
1 sugar cube
Ice cubes
2 oz/60 ml Old Overholt or other rye whiskey
2 dashes of Peychaud's bitters
1 lemon peel strip, for garnish

Rinse a rocks glass with the absinthe. Put the sugar cube in the bottom of a mixing glass, top with a few drops of water, and muddle together. Add ice, the whiskey, and bitters and stir until well chilled, about 15 seconds. Strain into the absinthe-rinsed glass. Twist the lemon peel over the glass to release its oils and then drop it into the drink before serving.

BROKEN BRANCH

David Nepove, San Francisco

This after-dinner drink is a great twist on the classic Manhattan. David created it to play two roles: a wonderfully complex cocktail that any bourbon lover will enjoy and a solid introduction to bourbon for newbies. It's got a sweeter flavor and a little less alcohol than the original, making it an easy first step into whiskey cocktails.

1½ oz/45 ml Knob Creek bourbon or other bourbon
½ oz/15 ml sweet vermouth
½ oz/15 ml maraschino liqueur
½ oz/15 ml Amaro Averna or other *amaro* such as Fernet Branca
Dash of Angostura bitters
Ice cubes
1 orange peel strip, for garnish

Combine the bourbon, vermouth, maraschino liqueur, *amaro*, and bitters in a mixing glass with ice and stir until well chilled, 20 to 30 seconds. Strain into a chilled cocktail glass. Garnish with the orange peel before serving.

LAUGHING WATER

Brooke Arthur, San Francisco

This is a great cocktail to impress. It's not made with the typical ingredients you'd find in colonial America, but it's got the same good ol' rye.

2 oz/60 ml Rittenhouse rye or other rye
¾ oz/25 ml Dolin or other dry vermouth
½ oz/15 ml fresh lemon juice
½ oz/15 ml Cinnamon Syrup (recipe follows)
¼ oz/10 ml fresh pineapple juice
Ice cubes
Nutmeg, for garnish

Combine the rye, vermouth, lemon juice, cinnamon syrup, and pineapple juice in a cocktail shaker with ice and shake vigorously until well chilled, about 20 seconds. Strain into a chilled coupe glass. Grate a pinch of nutmeg on top before serving.

CINNAMON SYRUP: In a saucepan, combine 1 cup/200 g sugar, 1 cup/240 ml water, and 4 cinnamon sticks and bring to a boil, stirring to dissolve the sugar. Boil for 5 minutes, then remove from the heat, cover, and let cool completely. Strain into a sealable bottle, cap, and refrigerate until cold and viscous before using. The syrup will keep for up to 2 weeks.

PANCHO AND LEFTY

Samir Osman, San Francisco

This cocktail was inspired by the country song of the same name. The song was sung by musician Merle Haggard, who happened to be the face of Dickel. Samir told me that he loves to mix spirits the same way country music stars pair cowboys and Mexicans. He took that inspiration and chose Dickel No. 12 to represent Lefty and Del Maguey Mezcal Vida to be Pancho. It's a drink with complex flavors: smoke and earthiness from the mezcal, acidity from the lemon juice, and richness from the whisky. In Samir's words, it's "definitely no wilting flower on the palate," and it's great to pair with hearty dishes or a classic country song.

2 oz/60 ml Dickel No. 12 whisky
½ oz/15 ml Del Maguey Mezcal Vida or other mezcal
½ oz/15 ml fresh lemon juice
½ oz/15 ml maple syrup
2 dashes of peach bitters
4 fresh sage leaves
Ice cubes

Combine the whisky, mezcal, lemon juice, maple syrup, bitters, and 3 of the sage leaves in a cocktail shaker with ice and shake vigorously until well chilled, 20 to 30 seconds. Strain into a small rocks glass and garnish with the remaining sage leaf before serving.

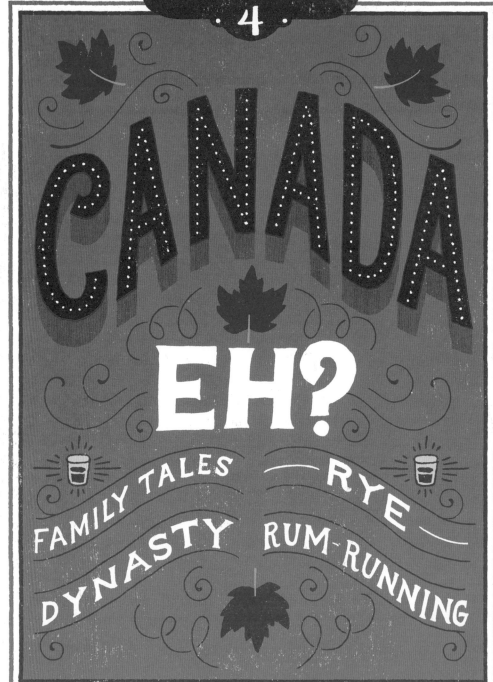

CHAPTER · 4 ·

CANADA

EH?

FAMILY TALES — RYE

DYNASTY RUM-RUNNING

All too often, Canada seems to get the short end of the hockey stick. Although it stands with the mightiest of the world powers, it's frequently upstaged by United States politics, culture, and reality TV shows. Jim Carrey, Pamela Anderson, and Ryan Gosling are all Canadian, but that fact got lost along the way. In the same manner, I've had Canadian whisky dozens of times and not even known it. Canada is on the charts as one of the world's major whisky-producing countries, and since you will always find Canadian whiskies at any decent bar and a bottle of CANADIAN CLUB on Don Draper's desk in *Mad Men*, it's well worth your acquaintance. The history of Canadian whisky is closely tied to that of its neighbor to the south, and as the region's whisky steps into the twenty-first century and showcases its mighty brands, it's clear that there is more to Canada than ice hockey and trees.

Whisky came to Canada around the same time that it made its way into the American colonies. In fact, there was no Canada yet; it was a British colony all the way until 1867. As immigrants started pouring into North America, boundaries were blurred and British settlements dotted the entire East Coast. The United States and Canada led parallel lives, and as they grew and became independent from Europe, their whiskies diverged into two distinct styles. Whisky distilling first took root in Canada in the Quebec area and gained support as British loyalists (and other nationals who didn't want the colonies to separate from the United Kingdom) fled the United States after the Revolutionary War. In the mid-1800s, Irish and Scottish immigrants headed to Canada in search of new opportunities and to escape the Irish famine. At one point, the area was a concentrated booze fest: Upper Canada had fifty-one licensed stills and only fifteen thousand residents. That would be like New York having more than five thousand stills in Manhattan alone. Canada was able to continue the development of its whisky industry unimpeded by the chaos of the Revolutionary War, the Civil War, and Prohibition experienced by its neighbor. In fact, the rough history of the United States fueled the unprecedented growth of the large Canadian distilleries and helped push the industry to new heights.

A TALE OF TWO FAMILIES

Two mega whisky empires represent the Canadian whisky industry, and they took their companies from domestic names to internationally renowned brands. Individually, HIRAM WALKER and SEAGRAM'S shaped the direction and defined the trends of Canadian whisky. Both used some of the most notable marketing campaigns the world has ever seen. Neither family is still behind the wheel, but the household names will always be synonymous with Canadian whisky.

Canadian Club (Hiram Walker)

Today, the name HIRAM WALKER sits on cheap bottles of sour watermelon schnapps and caramel apple liqueur, but Hiram himself is one of the grandfathers of Canadian whisky. No relation to Johnnie's whisky in Scotland, Hiram Walker was actually an American-born grocer who lived in Detroit. Excited by the prospect of making booze, he moved to Canada and started a distillery on the Detroit River in 1858. Walker's distillery became the backbone of a town that would later be named Walkerville, after its founder. He is credited with originating the light-style whisky Canada is known for and for bottling WALKER'S CLUB WHISKY, a popular drink in gentlemen's clubs in the mid to late 1800s. As several questionable legends have it, U.S.-based distillers, envious of Walker's success, prompted the passage of regulations that forced foreign distillers to label their products with their country of origin, and a rebranded CANADIAN CLUB (sometimes known as C. C.) was born that proved an even hotter commodity. The growth of CANADIAN CLUB continued long past Walker's death, and it has become one of the staple Canadian whiskies at bars across the globe. The brand hovers over James Dean's head in the famous snapshot taken in Times Square, and it was my grandfather's drink of choice.

The brand has worldwide fame and has run several notable advertising campaigns. In a Willy Wonka golden-ticket-style promotion, the company hid cases of whisky in inaccessible landmarks and remote territories. Many of the cases were found in extreme locations, from the summit of Mount Kilimanjaro to Death Valley to the top of a New York skyscraper. One was even found in the South Pacific island nation of Tonga in 2011. Several cases (including one in the Arctic Circle) have yet to be discovered. Good luck.

Crown Royal (Seagram's)

SEAGRAM'S was the other big player in the trajectory of Canadian whisky. Pioneered by Joseph Seagram, the budding company was handed to his sons, who later sold it to the legendary Bronfman family in 1928. The Bronfmans were Jewish immigrants from (what is now) Moldova who moved to Canada in 1889, with business prospects on their mind. They had a hand in everything from tobacco growing to hotel management to a successful mail-order booze business, but nothing compared with their success in selling whisky. Under Samuel Bronfman, the family dynasty guided SEAGRAM'S to exponential growth. He piloted the operation through years of U.S. Prohibition and dozens of acquisitions (including a few Scotch distilleries) to become the world's largest beverage company. It spawned several of the large brands that continue to be the pillars of Canadian whisky. Bronfman's son and grandson continued to grow the empire by buying up big shares of an oil company and Universal Studios. The company was eventually split up and its alcohol brands bought by other large corporate alcohol giants, but the Seagram's name still lives on in several whiskies, tonics, and sodas.

All of SEAGRAM'S flagship brands are blends and are perfect archetypes of the light-bodied Canadian style. CROWN ROYAL was created to honor Queen Elizabeth and George VI on their visit to Canada in 1939. It comes in the iconic crown-shaped bottle in a purple velvet casing that is ideal for any marble collection. The brand was available only in Canada for its first twenty-five years, but it has now become the number-one-selling Canadian whisky in the United States. Although many people think that SEAGRAM'S SEVEN CROWN is Canadian, it's actually made in the United States and is best known for mixing with 7UP to make a 7 and 7, a basic drink taught to all new bartenders. It's an easy step for drinkers who might have preferred a vodka soda.

PROHIBITION

Canada didn't suffer the same slings and arrows that the United States did from a federal prohibition, but it did have a strong temperance movement and a half-assed struggle to establish dry regions through the turn of the twentieth century. Prohibition officially took effect in Canada during World War I, but myriad exceptions to the rule (including making alcohol for export) made laws difficult to enforce, and it didn't last long. One can only imagine the French enclave of Quebec voting in a prohibition referendum; the French would never have it. *Vive la résistance!*

U.S. Prohibition dried up Canada's closest competition and helped create a massive market of thirsty consumers and opportunistic mobsters. With hundreds of local distilleries shut down, U.S. residents looked to Canada to get their fix. Although many of the smaller Canadian distilleries suffered, it was a golden time of growth for the country's two whisky giants. Canada got creative and managed to smuggle an endless supply of booze into the States. It was much nearer than Caribbean rum and easier to import than booze from Scotland. Carrying liquor across the Great Lakes became an easy way to make a few extra bucks, and rum-running was rampant. On a larger scale, Canadian distilleries exported whisky and turned a blind eye when shipments that left the country dropped off the radar. **Through a maze of different channels, a huge proportion of the whisky drunk in American cities during Prohibition flowed through Canada.** CANADIAN CLUB became one of the biggest moneymakers for mobsters, and the industry grew tremendously.

The two big Canadian whisky producers were perfectly poised for world domination following the repeal of Prohibition. They had amassed fortunes during America's Noble Experiment and were now cranking out colossal quantities for consumers who were already hooked. The minute that Prohibition was repealed, Canadian whisky was cheap, popular, and ubiquitous in every bar.

WHAT'S INSIDE?

Most Canadian whiskies fall closer to the American style of whiskey, and their flavors slide alongside bourbon rather than their Scottish counterparts. However, the manufacturing rules are much more lax than the strict guidelines for bourbon. As for specifics, Canadian whisky must be made in Canada (no shit), it must be aged at least three years, and natural flavors and colors can be added to it. There are no rules about what kind of barrels to use either, and many distilleries employ an eclectic mix of new oak and used sherry, bourbon, or other barrels. In the end, most of these whiskies are married together anyhow, so it's difficult to pull out individual tastes.

BLENDS

The vast majority of Canadian whiskies are blends. A base of virtually tasteless light grain whisky is aged and mixed with layers of flavoring whiskies that impart most of the taste. Nearly all of the large distilleries produce several kinds of base whiskies and various flavoring whiskies with the intention of blending or selling them in volume. The end products are usually fairly light and easy to drink. The small percentage of flavoring whisky is often made from rye, which has led to many Canadian whiskies being erroneously (by American standards) called rye whisky. More often than not, corn is actually the main ingredient in Canadian whisky. Whiskies like ALBERTA PREMIUM are anomalies in the bunch. It's made entirely from rye, which gives it a floral, drier, spicier physique.

The few leading brands from the 1900s continue to dominate the Canadian whisky market and make up the international face of the Canadian industry. Each of them shares similar smooth, light, mellow characteristics that make them great for mixed drinks. CANADIAN MIST and BLACK VELVET were both launched after Prohibition, and you'll be able to find either without having to open your eyes. Most of the prominent brands, like CROWN ROYAL and CANADIAN CLUB, have reserve or special editions that pitch to the demand for bolder flavors and small-batch whiskies. Keep an eye out for CANADIAN CLUB RESERVE and CROWN ROYAL'S RESERVE and CASK NO. 16.

SINGLE MALT

Of course, exceptions exist to any rule, and **GLENORA** is a Canadian single-malt distillery that looks like it was airlifted straight out of Scotland. Its location in a Celtic town where students learn Gaelic gives legitimacy to the region being called Nova Scotia (New Scotland). The distillery makes a few different styles of their **GLEN BRETON RARE**, one of Canada's only single malts (aged in ice-wine barrels). Seeing the word *Glen* on a bottle of Canadian whisky is reminiscent of Scotches and can be misleading, or at least so thought the Scotch Whisky Association. The naming of the whisky was a point of contention with the regulatory board for several years in the late 2000s, but the Canadian courts cleared the way for **GLENORA** to continue using the name. It was immigrants from Scotland who started the distillery in the first place, and four thousand kilometers couldn't keep them from recreating their native spirit. Fear not: if you're able to hunt down **GLEN BRETON RARE**, you'll see that it's got a large maple leaf on the front of the bottle, lest you forget where it's made.

THE FUTURE

Canadian whisky is the bestselling whisky in North America. It introduced Americans to smooth, easy drinking but lost some of its fame to an even smoother and easier drink with the advent of vodka. Although it took a while, Canadian whisky is back on the map.

Unfortunately, government regulations in Canada, similar to the one that is surging in the United States, limit the tide of craft distilling but a few microdistilleries are in the works. Independent companies like **FORTY CREEK** in Ontario are slowly planting themselves in Canadian soil, and other bottlers are diving into the Canadian whisky market. **Creativity is flowering in the land of the Mounties, but the whiskies don't often trickle out to other countries.** If you find yourself in any major Canadian city, head to a local whisky bar and see what kinds of surprises they can pour; a whisky flight might display some of Canada's finest. Boundaries are also blurring: U.S. brands like WHISTLEPIG are buying Canadian-rye flavoring whiskies to mix and bottle in Vermont. With renewed interest in single malts and craft products, a blizzard of new bottles will show up in the next several years. Just remember, above the international border, ordering a rye will be as vague as asking for a whisky. Innovative products like premixed canned cocktails and flavored whiskies are already making the rounds. Canada is catching the eye of a new generation of revelers, and although the Montreal Expos no longer exist, the country's whisky makers are stepping up to the plate.

While Canada is steadily producing spirits of higher quality, product placement in pop TV shows like *Mad Men* continues to boost sales of traditional labels, thrusting the country's whisky industry back into the international spotlight. During the 1950s, CANADIAN CLUB would have been the obvious choice to reach for in the middle of a stressful day at the office. It's light, easy, and you can find it anywhere. It's also the simplest way for me to celebrate my sparse Canadian roots. God save the Queen.

SCOFFLAW

With a name literally meaning someone who openly breaks the law, the drink was brought to life in New York during Prohibition.

1½ oz/45 ml Canadian Club whisky
1 oz/30 ml dry vermouth
½ oz/15 ml fresh lemon juice
¾ oz/25 ml grenadine
Dash of orange bitters
Ice cubes
1 lemon peel strip, for garnish

Combine the whisky, vermouth, lemon juice, grenadine, and bitters in a mixing glass with ice and stir until well chilled, 20 to 30 seconds. Strain into a chilled cocktail glass. Twist the lemon peel over the glass to release its oils and then drop it into the drink before serving.

THE COURT JESTER

Ford Mixology Lab, New York City

This is a modern version of the scofflaw. The recipe substitutes St-Germain elderflower liqueur for grenadine, giving the drink a more floral flavor. Ford Mixology Lab explained that the name is a shout-out to court jesters who would scoff at the laws of royalty.

2 oz/60 ml Crown Royal whisky
1 oz/30 ml dry vermouth
½ oz/15 ml fresh lemon juice
¼ oz/10 ml elderflower liqueur
2 dashes of grapefruit bitters
Ice cubes
1 orange peel strip, for garnish

Combine the whisky, vermouth, lemon juice, elderflower liqueur, and bitters in a cocktail shaker with ice and shake vigorously until well chilled, 20 to 30 seconds. Strain into a chilled coupe glass. Twist the orange peel over the glass to release its oils and then drop it into the drink before serving.

Or, for maximum effect and a nice smoky flavor, light a match, hold it just above the drink, and then hold the orange peel, colored-side down, just above the flame. Twist and pinch the peel to release the oils, which will ignite a nice flare, then toss the peel into the drink.

SASKATCHEWAN PUNCH

The Bon Vivants

This is a great punch to sip on during those cold Canadian nights in front of the fire with Pamela Anderson. The ingredient amounts are expressed as parts so you can make as much or as little as you like.

1 part Canadian Club Sherry Cask whisky

¾ part Leopold New York sour apple liqueur

¾ part Hidalgo Oloroso sherry

¾ part pomegranate juice

½ part fresh lemon juice

1 part steeped black tea

2 dashes Angostura bitters

½ part Quatre-Épice Honey Syrup (recipe follows)

1 large block of ice

Thin apple slices for garnish

Combine all the liquid ingredients in a punch bowl. Place the block of ice into the bowl, which will chill the punch without over-diluting. Add in the apple slices. Serve with a ladle into punch cups.

QUATRE-ÉPICE HONEY SYRUP: In a small saucepan, combine 8 oz/225 g honey, 8 oz/225 g sugar, and 8 oz/240 ml water. In a small sauté pan, toast 10 whole cloves, 1 cinnamon stick, 3 whole star anise pods, and 2 tsp allspice berries until the aromas fill the room and then add them to the honey mixture. Bring to a boil and let simmer for about 5 minutes until the sugar has completely dissolved. Remove from the heat and let cool. Transfer the mixture to a covered container and refrigerate overnight to fully infuse the spices. Strain through a fine-mesh sieve and discard the spices. The syrup will keep in the refrigerator for 3 to 4 weeks.

CHAPTER 5

Scotland!

WHAT'S UNDER THE KILT?

In the world of whisky, Scotch reigns. It is the most widely known and most revered whisky in the world, and it is, quite literally, the drink of kings and queens. Much of its early history predates the United States, and its development in the British Isles paved the road for what you drink at your local bar. If you enjoy Scotch and care to learn anything about it, make some time in your busy life to go to Scotland. Rolling hills, snaking rivers, legendary monsters, and majestic castles help to crown the region as one of the most beautiful places on Earth. Scotland is, by all accounts, a Disneyland for adults. Throw on a kilt, replace Mickey with famed Scottish poet Robert Burns, and ditch your funnel cake for haggis and after a few drams, you won't know what hit you. Keep one thing in mind, however: **If you find yourself at a bar in Scotland, don't be caught ordering a Scotch. In these parts, it's just called whisky.**

Whisky was not a Scottish invention. In fact, the Scots stole it from their Irish neighbors, hijacked it as their own, and mastered it long ago. Now it's one of the United Kingdom's top exports and a product that is mimicked worldwide. Even hundreds of years ago, homemade booze was commonplace. Nay, it was rampant. Barley grew well in the northern climate, and locals were dreaming up ways to use excess grains and stay warm through the dark, cold winters.

As soon as James IV (1488—1513) caught on to the distilling going on in his country, he licensed a monopoly to manufacture the whisky to keep it flowing. Production increased and the spirit was regulated, but many more farmers made illegal booze. Whisky was first taxed in 1644, and shortly after, illegal distilleries popped up around the country. A monarchy needs a high, steady cash flow to keep producing crowns, scepters, and ruby-studded goblets, and whisky was liquid gold. Tax collection turned out to be a messy business, and many small distillers proved unwilling to pay taxes on their native spirit, resorting to smuggling and other unlawful activities to avoid the excisemen.

A couple of hundred years later, George IV fell in love with GLENLIVET and pushed Scotch into the spotlight, easing a path for legalization of underground distilleries, widespread licensing, and eventual mass exportation. Under his rule, the taxation system became clearer and many whisky makers made their way over to legal distilling. As other small companies began to slide into the budding whisky industry, businesses grew beyond their greatest expectations. Many Brits were big consumers of sherry, port, and Cognac, but they turned to whisky after Europe's grape industry was hit by a blight caused by insects in the 1850s. The outspoken love of whisky from writers like Charles Dickens further fueled a growing demand.

Although Prohibition was a dark and completely destructive fourteen years for the American bourbon industry, it helped grow an international Scotch market. Because of its medicinal smell, LAPHROAIG Scotch legally made its way into doctors' prescriptions in the United States. It was an exception, however, and most Scotch came in undercover. A succession of illegal importers headed to Europe in search of partners willing to smuggle in whisky to quench America's thirst. As the story goes (and for many reasons, still remains fuzzy), the chain of command flowed through Al Capone and the mob directly to JFK's father, Joseph Kennedy. Since Kennedy was Irish American, the Americans naturally went to Ireland first to line up their supply of whisky. The Irish distilleries refused to participate in illegal shenanigans, however, so the Americans headed over to Scotland, where whisky makers were more than happy to sell their wares. As it played out, the day after Prohibition ended, Joseph Kennedy's company,

Somerset Importers, was granted the exclusive importing rights to **DEWAR'S SCOTCH**. He consequently made millions in the years that followed. And so goes beautiful American democracy.

The rebirth of the bourbon industry after Prohibition had profound effects on the development of Scotch. Perhaps the most notable was access to used bourbon barrels for maturing whisky. Newfound availability of American barrels couldn't have happened at a better time. Sherry casks were becoming more difficult to acquire during the Spanish Civil War. The use of secondhand barrels from bourbon producers changed the face of an industry that for years had relied on wood soaked with port, sherry, or other wine.

The Scotch industry grew with an emerging U.S. market but had turbulent times and big changes ahead. Whisky making became more mechanized in the 1960s, through a series of transformations. First, distilleries turned away from using coal to heat their stills (but only after several distilleries burned down). To grow economies of scale, distilleries bought barley from central malting plants, which, in turn, helped create greater consistency among single malts from season to season. Machinery started moving toward the fully automated and computerized systems that most companies now use. **Today, many distilleries have only two people running the show at any moment, one checking on equipment and the other sitting behind a computer monitoring everything as if it were a game of FarmVille.** Further changes happened after the oil crisis in the 1970s, when production took a steep downturn and a wave of distilleries closed. The industry has since made a large U-turn, and the renewed interest in Scotch is opening doors and firing up stills for a new era of production. Today, more than twenty-five hundred brands of Scotch are sold around the world.

WHAT'S IN A NAME?

The naming of spirits in the United Kingdom is both a cultural trend and a legal labyrinth that has molded the identity of Scotch. A series of laws and decrees, the most recent of which was set into motion in 2009, established guidelines for making and marketing the spirit. Although many lawyers seem to be whisky drinkers, the legal wording of the regulations is drier than Scotch itself. In practice, the laws exist to make sure you're guaranteed a minimum standard of quality. The regulations stop your neighbor from distilling old orange juice, adding some artificial flavors, and selling it as whisky—a concoction that might not only put you off from learning more about Scotch but also kill you. You can jump online to read the full text of the Scotch Whisky Act, but the important pieces are (1) the spirit must be made in Scotland, (2) the spirit must age in a barrel for at least three years, and (3) the final product must have no flavor additives. So, if you were hoping for cannabis-flavored Scotch to appear on the market, you may just have to wait until Prince Harry becomes king.

STYLES AND WHAT MATTERS WHEN DRINKING

It's difficult to pinpoint the flavor of Scotch. It can range from the lightest, gentlest sweet fruit to the heaviest medicinal seawater, making it unfeasible to categorize all the styles under one umbrella. A handful of decisions made in production can vastly change the character of Scotch even within each distillery. Some decisions carry big weight, like whether the whisky should be peaty and smoky and how much so. Other decisions will give the Scotch more subtle flavors that are shades of color in the final painting. These factors make each whisky unique and help to tickle your brain with euphoric delight or drive you to rip out your tongue.

Remember, all whiskies are made from just three simple ingredients, water, yeast, and grain, so knowing the fundamental decisions that distillers make when combining these ingredients will help you ask the right questions. Being able to discuss whiskies with gusto and with attention to detail, such as citing the specific yeast strain or the shape of the condenser on a still, will make you sound like a complete and utter whisky geek. And if you do, more power to you.

Here is a short list of the major decisions that affect every bottle of whisky: (1) grains, peat, barrel, age; (2) fermentation, yeast; and (3) shape of still, small decisions. The easiest way to understand what you are drinking would be to concentrate on the items under number one. Every piece of the whisky-making process can change a spirit's flavor and aroma, however, from the shape and metal of the still to the material of the fermentation tanks and the type of barley, so if you find yourself interested in learning about the items under numbers two and three, make your way to Geeking Out on page 154.

Grains

In Scotch, barley is king. Mark Reynier, the one-time owner of the BRUICHLADDICH (pronounced *brook-lad-dee*) distillery, explained barley as having "mind-fucking complexity." It makes whisky the most complex and interesting spirit in the world. Malted barley will often contribute the deep, complex, umami-like rounded flavor to whisky and is thus the coveted ingredient in most Scotch. Barley is like Kobe beef: it can be ground up with other meat to make a delicious hamburger, but it has much more intense flavor if served by itself. Like other whiskies, Scotch can also be made using corn, wheat, or rye. Each grain will bring subtle nuances to the table, but unless we're talking barley, the types of grain in Scotch are rarely spoken about. A simplified classification of Scotch into single malts and blends will help you maneuver around most bottles.

Single Malts

As explained in chapter 1, a single malt is made entirely from a single malted grain at a single distillery. Since malted barley is king, if we're talking single-malt Scotch, we're talking about barley. The craving for more interesting tastes and the desire to know the origins of your food and drink have given way to the exponential growth of single malts. I know you know single malts. You get them for your boss at Christmas and your uncles are asking for them during the holidays. They are the subject of a tsunami of online conversations and niche tastings. Single malt is also a sexy buzzword, and I've met confused consumers who say they like single malts but would never put their hands on Scotch. Dear non–Scotch drinker, you are a Scotch drinker.

Since barley was common, the first whiskies produced in Scotland would have undoubtedly fallen into the single-malt classification. The resurgence and hype about single malts, however, is a relatively recent phenomenon, hitting the world stage in a big way in the 1980s. A perfect storm of economic conditions and consumers' changing palates led to an excess of Scotch. Rather than spending extra time and money creating blends, they released a flood of single malts onto the market. In an era when dozens of distilleries were shutting their doors, the food revolution was picking up steam and movements like Slow Food were helping to build interest in single malts. Our country had come a long way from the days of TV dinners and light whiskies. Sushi restaurants were popping up everywhere and foodies were becoming fussy about what they drank. Because single malts must come from a single distillery, it's easy to know a lot about the spirit you're knocking back. With that additional knowledge, the whisky geek was born. Like knowing that your eggs come from a chicken named Margaret who roamed freely at Green Park Farms, you also know that your OBAN single malt was made from malted barley across the alleyway from a little Chinese restaurant in the town of Oban. I can show you a photo of the machinery that made your whisky and could probably write a short biography on the history of your drink. No more anonymous whisky.

Single malts stepped up to the podium at the end of the twentieth century, and spotlights are still shining bright. Although they continue to account for less than 10 percent of all the Scotch sold worldwide, they are the fastest-growing segment of the industry. Wealth at the top of the pyramid is increasing; expensive single malts are swirling excitement around the prospect of richer, more flavorful alternatives to the usual fare.

To make a single malt, a distillery often mixes, or "marries," a bunch of different whiskies (all malted barley) to create the end flavor. As long as it all happens at one distillery, it's still single malt. Distillers hate using the word *blending* because it's confused with other blended whiskies, but that's what they're doing; they're just keeping it in the family. A single malt from GLEN GRANT, for example, could be a mix of dozens of different barrels of whisky that were made at the distillery and have been aging in casks for a range of years. The final creation—a single malt—has a unique taste that was designed by a master blender. Most single-malt distilleries send the bulk of their whisky off to become one of the many flavors in big blends. With few exceptions, the name on the bottle of a single malt is also the name of the distillery.

Don't drink single malts for the short-term goal of getting buzzed. There are much cheaper ways to do that. If a whisky is made entirely out of barley (hint: single malt), the bottle will tell you. If a bottle says nothing, it's a blend.

Sir Mix-a-lot

If making whisky is chemistry, blending is an art. The vast majority of the Scotch imbibed around the world is blended. A blended Scotch can be made from malted barley with any other grains and can be a mixture of whiskies from any number of distilleries. With the arrival of technological innovations around 1830 that allowed for quick mass production of lighter grain whisky, blends proved to be a much cheaper way to make shiploads of whisky. A large industrial grain distillery can make as much whisky in a week as a small malt distillery like TALISKER makes in a year. Grain spirits make up the base of blended Scotches (usually anywhere from 10 to 70 percent of the mix), and single malts add most of the flavor to the end product. Grain whisky is the canvas, and malt whisky is the paint that creates the picture. As a general rule, production techniques result in lighter grain blends with less intense flavors than their single-malt counterparts. That's why you may have seen connoisseurs snub their noses at blends. Approach them with an open mind. They can sometimes surprise you.

Back in the day, when booze was mostly sold at local grocery stores in Scotland, customers would fill up their ceramic jars from a cask of whisky. Somewhere between the bushels of peas and the mounds of chicken gizzards, grocers in the countryside started making blended whiskies. The most famous blender was a boy named Johnnie Walker, who got his start mixing teas at his family's market. He later started playing around with the barrels of whisky at the shop, mixing them into his own creations. Blending whiskies was a way for him and other grocers to give customers more consistency and offer their own twist on local booze. Johnnie's Scotch has been selling since the early 1800s, and after he purchased a few distilleries to supply whisky for his blends, the Walker family led the brand for decades of impressive growth. Fueled by a brilliant marketing campaign and international fame, the eponymous blends are still among the top-selling whiskies of the world. Some of the current JOHNNIE WALKER labels are made with a mix of up to fifty different whiskies. You'll never know the entire makeup of any blends because the brands don't want them copied, but know that they were a very intentional mix of tastes on the part of the blenders. Using fifty-plus distilleries also ensures consistency. A distiller making a single malt has a narrow color wheel of whiskies from one distillery, but blenders don't need to limit themselves, as they can work with a much wider spectrum of flavors. **If a single malt is a group of violinists with a brilliant tone, a blend might be the full orchestra.** By following a recipe of barrels from different distilleries, blenders are trained to make massive quantities that match the taste of the batch that preceded it. It's the blender's job to ensure that your whisky tastes identical bottle to bottle, no matter where you drink it.

Most of the big names in Scotch are blends. Any whisky you get on a plane is most likely a blend; most well drinks will be made with blended whisky. For reference, all bottles of JOHNNIE WALKER are blends, CHIVAS REGAL is a blend, and so are most DEWAR'S, GRANT'S, and FAMOUS GROUSE bottles. It's not difficult to find out some of the single-malt whiskies that go into blends. GLENROTHES is the big single malt in the CUTTY SARK blend, FAMOUS GROUSE has HIGHLAND PARK in it, and CHIVAS REGAL gets one of its many pillars from STRATHISLA single malt.

Blends are for drinking, while single malts are for tasting. If you're going for a night of drinking and want to mix some whisky with Coke, don't go for the top shelf bottle of single malt; its subtle nuances will get lost in the caramel, high-fructose corn syrup, and carbonation. If you want to taste your way through the Scottish countryside, reach for single malts. Of course, you can also grab expensive and rare malts to impress your coworkers, but it's easy to integrate Scotch into your everyday life with less expensive blends. The Spanish love drinking whisky and Coke. Even the operations manager of the **CARDHU** distillery (one of the key single malts in the **JOHNNIE WALKER** blends) loves drinking **JOHNNIE WALKER RED LABEL** with tomato juice and Tabasco. A Bloody Mary Queen of Scots, anyone?

Scottish drinkers primarily drink blends. In fact, the most common and widely drunk whisky at Scottish bars is **FAMOUS GROUSE**, a relatively inexpensive blend that is a solid buy at the local pub for two pounds. Some occasions necessitate single malts, others are for blends, and every once in a while, it's time for an ice-cold beer. In the words of the manager of **CARDHU** distillery, "Just because I like venison, it doesn't mean I want to eat it every night."

This classification should not be read as a hierarchy. Just because a particular Scotch is a single malt, it doesn't mean that you'll like it best. The goal is for you to find what you enjoy drinking and taste everything along the way.

Peat and Repeat

A big element in Scotch is the peat flavor. That's the smoky, often harsh chemical flavor that turns a lot of people off on their first taste of Scotch. Like any stinky cheese or bitter beer, it's an acquired taste that may take a few drams to get used to, and maybe even years to crave. The flavor is a conscious decision to smoke some of the barley before it goes into making the whisky. Whereas you would use wood to smoke salmon (of which you can find a lot in Scotland), you use decayed vegetation called peat to smoke barley for Scotch. The bigger the percentage of barley smoked with peat, the more intense the smoky taste will be in the final whisky. Luckily, there's an actual science to it, so the distiller can get their desired level of "peatiness," and you can troll through the range of flavors.

Peat is not only useful for its taste, however. It is also a renewable energy source that is rich in oil and is cut straight out of the ground. Since it is simply decayed moss and grass, it was (and continues to be) a free and abundant resource in remote areas of Scotland. Traditionally, peat cutters made about one pound for every twenty-five square meters they cut. It is a simple technique that I mastered in twenty minutes, but nowadays most peat is harvested by machine. The old-fashioned way is to jam a spade into the wet ground, carefully lift out each brick of peat, and then leave it to dry. When wet, peat looks like oily mud; when dry, it looks like nothing more than arid chunks of dirt. Endless fields of peat on the Scottish island of Islay are saturated with rainwater and squish as you walk across them. They make for incredible scenery and the world capital for peated whiskies.

Although many people associate Scotch with the peat flavor, there's plenty of whisky being made in Scotland that is smoke free. As technology and access to alternative energy sources changed during the Industrial Revolution, many distilleries turned to hot air or coal to dry out their barley to stop the germination process. Unfortunately, very few bottles of Scotch tell you on the label whether they use peated barley and how much. You've got to open them up or read tasting notes to find out. Interestingly, most blends have at least a little peated whisky in them. It's like salt on potatoes. You might not consciously realize it, but it sure makes the potatoes taste better.

If you're not in love with the flavor of peated whiskies, that's totally fine. It's just a matter of preference. If you want to slide into them, take your time with them. Love can be learned, and you'll need to get your toes wet first. No need to go out and buy bottles of **BRUICHLADDICH'S OCTOMORE**, the most heavily peated whisky in the world. You may also want to wait to jump into a single malt from **LAPHROAIG**, which often comes with tasting notes like iodine, leather, and burnt rubber. It is, however, one of the favorite whiskies of Prince Charles and has received a royal warrant to supply the royal family. He has visited the distillery several times and his insignia appears on every bottle.

There are many brands that use peat in moderation and deliver a subtler hint of smoke. Once you become a peat freak, it's difficult to go back. To someone who always drinks big-bodied Scotches that drip of fires and burnt logs, other whiskies invariably lack oomph. There is a place and a time for each one. It's not worth starting off your dinner with a heavily peated single malt. It will only scar your taste buds and steer your meal into the asphalt. Peated whiskies are, however, a really nice way to finish a meal. One of my favorite simple peated cocktails is the Islay Campfire at Nopa restaurant in San Francisco. Perfect for a fog-chilled evening, it's a mix of espresso, **ARDBEG 10**, and coffee liqueur. If only we had those at summer camp.

If you're totally new to peated whisky, it is a good idea to taste some of the heavily peated brands so you know how far the flavor can go. Then take steps back until you hit something that strikes your fancy. My first super-peated whisky was an

ARDBEG SUPERNOVA: intense gunpowder-like smoke on a massively bodied beast. It blew my mind and threw my world off course. Now I crave it occasionally, and it's clear that peat can become an addiction.

Like people, peat mellows with age. The older a whisky is, the more the chemical peat flavor will relax into the background. Woody flavors take over with time and the mix of the two can bring the whisky together in a Zen-like balance.

Wood

Scotch spends the majority of its life locked away in a barrel. The wood gives it more than 60 percent of its flavor, all of its color, and most of its aroma. Since Scotch producers use only second-hand barrels, the quality, age, and previous purpose of the wood can have drastic effects on the end flavor of the whisky. If the barrel had sherry in it, the whisky is going to have a slight taste of sherry. If it had bourbon in it, you guessed it: it's going to taste a bit more like America. It's not such a subtle science, even though it sounds like a technicality. The barrels actually have some of their old contents stuck inside the wood, so a trace amount of bourbon actually makes its way into the Scotch.

Bourbon and sherry barrels are the most common in Scotland, but distilleries will reach for all sorts of used casks: port, Madeira, Sauternes, and Cognac. A few even age their whiskies in Caribbean rum barrels. Single malts are often a mix of whisky from several different casks, and many brands will tell you what the Scotch was finished in, giving a clue as to how the whisky tastes. **If a bottle only says the whisky was aged in oak casks, they're using vague bullshit marketing lingo. Remember, Scotch is *always* aged in oak.**

How Old Are Ya?

Seeing a row of numbers like 12, 15, 18, 21, 25, 30, and 35 at the liquor store can turn into an impossible Sudoku puzzle. They are all whisky ages, but it doesn't all add up why some bottles are three times more expensive or twice as dark as the ones next to them. For starters, older whiskies tend to be more expensive (check out chapter 1), but price and age are not a good indication of taste. You might love the 12-year-old and hate the 15-year-old. In fact, they may taste like two fundamentally different drinks. The number is the age of the youngest whisky in the bottle. An 18-year-old single-malt Scotch could easily have some 19-, 20-, or 35-year-old whisky mixed into the batch. If there is even a drop of 18-year-old, the bottle must be labeled as such. Age affects Scotch in all sorts of ways. The longer a Scotch sits in the barrel, the more it will taste like wood.

Just as older doesn't necessarily mean better, the color of Scotch is not indicative of age. Since Scotch ages in used barrels, blenders have a wide range of different woods at their disposal. As I have just explained, the specific casks (and what was last in them) will help dictate the distinct color, taste, and aroma. Take the nature versus nurture argument for a moment. A 12-year-old Scotch and a 15-year-old Scotch from a single distillery have the same DNA. By *nature* they are identical and were started off as the same liquid. The two whiskies are then *nurtured* in two very unique barrels and come out significantly different from each other. It's easiest to think of age statements as different styles rather than a ranking system. Just because you like the 12-year-old OLD PULTENEY doesn't mean you'll like the distillery's 17-year-old more. Check out bottles of the 12-year-old and the 15-year-old MACALLAN; the 12 is significantly darker than the 15 because it was aged in sherry barrels, which tend to turn whisky a darker red. Although the 15 is older, it spent more time in used bourbon casks, which give it a lighter color. It tastes noticeably different, too. The packaging is even coded accordingly: the sherry-colored box for the sherry finish. To make matters even trickier, it's perfectly legal for Scotch makers to add natural caramel color to get a desired tint.

Scotland's year-round chilly climate allows Scotch to mature longer than whisky that ages in the heat of Kentucky or Tennessee. Whereas most bourbon is bottled after 4 to 10 years of aging, Scotches are commonly 10 to 30 years old. Scotch takes more time to get the necessary flavor out of the wood barrel, but still, too long in wood is a bad thing. When I visited a castle in Speyside, Scotland, I had a small dram of **GLENURY ROYAL** 50-year-old. It was incredible diving into the most expensive whisky I've ever had, which was born the same year as my father, but it had hints of the inside drawer of an antique wooden desk—perhaps the most expensive desk I've ever tasted.

When it comes to solving a Sudoku, it's all about figuring out the number that fits the space. If you're sliding your credit card to get a bottle to enjoy with friends, figure out what flavors strike your fancy and go from there. If you're trying to impress your boss, go for the oldest. That's just the way the world works.

NAVIGATING THE MARKETPLACE

Scotch can be confusing. There are countless brands from all over Scotland, and to enter the world of Scotch can be like stepping into an enchanted forest and forgetting which direction is up. Independent bottlers, which comprise an entire curated arena of Scotch, can help point you in the right direction. So, too, can studying up on the regions where Scotch is made.

Independent Bottlers

Lucky for us, a handful of independent bottlers have taken on the role of expert tour guide and can help us navigate obscure single malts on the market. These companies generally don't make their own whisky but instead buy up individual casks from other established distilleries and either bottle them straight from the barrel or mix them together to make their own blends. That means that each and every bottle should shine because each barrel is handpicked.

One of the most interesting independent bottlers, **THE SCOTCH MALT WHISKY SOCIETY**, sprang up as an icon in the growing trend of single malts and has undoubtedly fueled its growth. It's a VIP whisky club with a paid membership, high-end lounges, and its own whisky magazine. Saying they know their Scotch is an understatement. Started by a couple of entrepreneurial single-malt fanatics in the 1970s, the society is a private group that buys single casks from distilleries around the world and bottles them under its own label. It has grown to more than twenty-five thousand members worldwide, with fifteen franchises around the globe.

The society has its own numerical naming convention that signifies the distillery and batch but does not label the whiskies by where they were made. A panel in the society selects barrels of single malts from around the world. Its members meet to sniff and taste their way through hundreds of samples and ultimately rate each one, giving it a thumbs up or thumbs down. The only clue as to what you're drinking is a series of tasting notes written by the panel. They'll try it neat and try it with a little water. Since the society does not blend whiskies or add anything to the whisky before it is bottled, the panel judges the single malts just as they come. Each barrel the panel agrees on has to be fit to carry the group's seal of approval.

The panel looks for barrels that make you sit up and take notice. It could be a 5-year-old whisky or a 45-year-old whisky, one that sings when you sip it or one that has the most unusual taste you've ever experienced. One of the panelists mentioned a tasting in which the participants stuck their noses into one of the samples and sniffed in silence for a full twenty minutes. The whisky was the oldest thing in the room, but even after their olfactory exhaustion, the taste didn't stand up to its aroma. Realizing that it would be more expensive than a case of other whiskies, the judges gave it thumbs down. Since all of the society's bottles look identical except for numerical identification, consumers are forced to set aside any prejudging based on branding, bottling, or age statements. Unless I scour the Internet for distillery listings, the only thing I know about Cask Number 93.46 is that it tastes like "tar, tea chests, and engine oil." It is whisky for whisky's sake.

Other independent bottlers can also serve as guides and pave any road to delightful drams of whisky. Unless the bottle is coming from **THE SCOTCH MALT WHISKY SOCIETY**, it will give you a good deal of information about what's inside. Sometimes the label will tell you when the whisky was distilled and when it was bottled, leaving you to do the math to figure out its age. **CADENHEAD'S** is an independent bottling company that has been around for more than 150 years, so it must be picking some damn good barrels. Britain's oldest spirit merchant, **BERRY BROS. & RUDD**, was established more than three hundred years ago and hand selects individual casks to bottle and sell. I would trust the company's insight. **If you can afford it, find an independent bottler whose taste in whisky you trust, and you'll always have a new whisky waiting for you.**

Regionality

You don't always have a curated whisky experience from independent bottlers at your disposal, and when you're on your own, it's all about knowing the foundations for Scotch and finding your way. Knowing a bit about the specific Scotch regions can be your personal compass rose to understanding what's in the bottle.

Somewhere up on the foggy, winding, scenic roads of Scotland, it's possible to spot the edge of the world. Isolation is an understatement. It's in many of these far corners and crevices that distilleries make some of the best whisky known to mankind. It's unfathomable to think that bottles get shipped from these small towns to lounges in Shanghai and boardrooms in Johannesburg. Nearly a hundred whisky distilleries are in operation, and most of them are far from urban civilization. They pepper the landscape, and it seems like the roads were built for their existence. Who in their right mind would have built HIGHLAND PARK and SCAPA distilleries on Orkney, one of the most remote areas of Scotland? Rivers and lochs (you've got to spit up some phlegm to say that correctly) crisscross the countryside. There's water everywhere in Scotland and land is plentiful; destinations clearly weren't scouted solely for their resources.

An interesting history hails from TALISKER, past the grazing sheep on the Isle of Skye. When you're procrastinating on Google Maps, look it up; it's far from the nearest city. Somewhere between the brink of civilization and Loch Ness, the majestic Isle of Skye (whose name in Old Norse means "misty isle") has weather that is worse than a San Francisco summer. In 1830, two brothers were looking to start a lucrative sheep business, so they decided to build the distillery on the island. In order to pull the local farmers off the land, the brothers employed them in their whisky business.

TALISKER, as with some other distilleries, was built as nothing more than a diversion to achieve two brothers' dreams of woolly riches. Everything at the distillery, except the abundance of natural ground water, is carried in and carried out. Before the network of one-lane thoroughfares was built, all ingredients came in via boat. The lifeline to the distillery was a small railway that ran from a dock on the nearby loch to the grain house (apparently the track remains a locomotive relic visited by people who obsess over old train history). Although it's a strange reason to put a distillery on the Isle of Skye, no one was going to move it after realizing that the fruited, peppery, peated whisky was delicious. Other distillery locations were chosen for various reasons: proximity to ports and railroads for export, nearness to barley fields, or generational family traditions.

Without fail, every time I step into a room mobbed with Scotch drinkers, I overhear tipsy murmurs of regional preferences. Traditionally, areas of Scotland made whisky in specific styles with identifiable flavors. It was a great way to categorize distilleries in our limited mental capacity. It's still the popular way to oversimplify and broadly understand nuanced styles, but the regionality—or *terroir*, if you will—is becoming a blurred generalization that doesn't hold up in modern-day whisky making. It pushes along a common language to discuss Scotch and is one of the few tools we have to group bottles of whisky together in categories. **But regionality in Scotland is a fluid concept, and what has been explained as seven regions can also be classified as six, five, or even four.** The most basic way to understand the layout and distribution of Scotch distilleries is in the five regions that follow. This is not a hard-and-fast formula, and if someone feels compelled to explain it differently, let him give his spiel.

Lowlands

Whiskies said to be from the Lowlands are made in the southern part of Scotland in distilleries close to the country's two major cities, Edinburgh and Glasgow. Where there were once more than twenty whisky distilleries, there are currently only three: AUCHENTOSHAN, GLENKINCHIE, and BLADNOCH. These whiskies are generally touted as light, fruity, and approachable.

Highlands

The Highlands region is virtually anything in the northern part of Scotland. It's a broad swatch and the vast majority of Scotch distilleries fall in this area, among them OBAN, ARDMORE, DALMORE, BEN NEVIS (which sits at the foot of Britain's highest mountain), and several more Glens: GLENMORANGIE, GLEN GARIOCH, GLEN ORD, and GLENGOYNE. Highland whiskies typically have richer fruit and floral flavors and are more robust than whiskies from the Lowlands.

Speyside

Technically a slice of the Highlands, Speyside is home to roughly half of Scotland's distilleries. They aren't piled together in a megaplex, but they're minutes apart as the woodcock flies. This region gets its name from the River Spey, a five-hundred-mile-long (the traditional Scottish mile is a little longer than the U.S. mile) salmon-filled river that winds through the highest concentration of whisky distilleries in the world. They all use similar ground water in their malts and employ the river water as coolant in production. Among the distilleries in the region are ARDMORE, BALVENIE, MACALLAN, CRAGGANMORE, CARDHU, GLENROTHES, GLENFARCLAS, GLENLIVET, and GLENFIDDICH. *Glen* simply means "valley," and that's where distilleries were often started—near a water source. The range of Speyside whiskies usually falls in the spectrum of grassy to richer, fruitier flavors. This region is home to the world's most popular single malts.

Islay

This is a region unto itself. Islay (pronounced eye-luh) is a landmark in the Scotch world and a Mecca for peat lovers. Part of the Inner Hebrides archipelago off the coast of mainland Scotland, Islay is covered with damp, soft green peat bogs and friendly folks who honk hello as they pass one another on the narrow road. Since the island is a destination for whisky drinkers around the world, summers host thousands of tourists clambering to see the birthplace of their favorite malts. The landscape is sprinkled with iconic white-walled distilleries and small towns, and the island seems to have more sheep enjoying its lush fields than it has people. This is the home of ARDBEG, LAPHROAIG, BRUICHLADDICH, BOWMORE, CAOL ILA, LAGAVULIN, BUNNAHABHAIN, and KILCHOMAN. Driving around the island is a majestic experience, with double rainbows that link fuzzy green knolls to wooden fishing docks on the water's edge. It's a quiet corner of the country and the air is the freshest I've ever had in my lungs.

There is no standing rule that Islay whiskies must follow a specific style, but most are very peaty, smoky, and briny and some even have chemical undertones. If you're interested in diving into the Islay whiskies, try a range of them side by side. A comparative approach will help you identify unique tastes when faced with their intensity. Getting into a whisky like LAPHROAIG usually takes training, as it's known for its burnt rubber, smoke, and iodine flavors. Exceptions to the rule exist, and a few lighter styles are coming off the island, including BUNNAHABHAIN's single malts. On the whole, Islay malts represent one of the fastest-growing segments of the Scotch industry.

Why so many distilleries on Islay? Its proximity to Ireland made it a natural first step in the historical journey of whisky. Traveling the twenty-five-mile journey from northern Ireland, whisky makers found a fertile island that was perfect for growing barley, cutting peat, and loading barrels of whisky onto boats to ship world-wide. Ever since those early years, generations have been carrying on the whisky tradition and basking in the beauty of the island.

Islands

This is a strange classification because it's not much of a region at all. It tosses together the rest of the distilleries around Scotland that don't quite fit into the other categories. Distilleries that get grouped here include **TALISKER** on the Isle of Skye, **HIGHLAND PARK** and **SCAPA** up in the northernmost part of the country (Orkney), and distilleries on the Islands of Arran and Jura. Whiskies in this category are usually smoky and briny and fall somewhere between the Scotches of the Highlands and the peat bombs of Islay. Single malts from an area called Campbeltown are similar in style to the whiskies of these Islands distilleries, though the peninsula off the west coast of Scotland actually used to be its own region. Campbeltown was a powerhouse of whisky production with more than thirty distilleries, but only three remain.

As with the rest of the whisky regions, Islands style is only a generalization. Several of these distilleries rarely make peated whiskies, and no guidelines exist for making any specific flavors. If you're intrigued but don't know where to start, dive into a **HIGHLAND PARK 12**. It's an elegantly balanced peated whisky that is a great introduction to Islands life.

Most of the distilling communities in all the regions are tightly knit towns of whisky makers and their families; workers know one another well. On my way out of Islay, I found myself on a small propeller plane with the entire ten-person staff of the ARDBEG distillery. There was a warm familial connection among them and a genuine love for what they do. These ten people represent a brand that has a football-like cult following from Moscow to Minnesota, and they had enormous pride in their work. Life on Islay is as interconnected as you would expect in any small town, and many spouses and parents have worked at competing distilleries. Although I'm not supposed to mention it, the distilleries even lend one another equipment and occasionally offer advice. While companies are fighting for space behind the bar on an international level, on the ground, there's still good ol' Scottish camaraderie. On an island with a population of fewer than four thousand, there's no room for sabotage. **It's all about sharing the dram and living the dream.**

TRENDS

As mentioned earlier, the single malt is the fastest-growing segment of the Scotch market. It's got the sexiness and the intrigue that continues to capture whisky drinkers worldwide. It has become a game of tasting as many as possible and finding the rare ones from distilleries that no longer exist (this can make bottles both rare and expensive, since there is a limited and dwindling supply). People want more than ever to taste a moment in time and explore single malts with an unbridled enthusiasm never before seen in the whisky world.

The Scotch industry is gravitating toward a younger population, and the whisky world is becoming less pretentious. With the recognition that intimidated drinkers are not loyal consumers, whisky companies are courting a new force of Generation Y social-media mavens. Whereas several years ago distillers would have balked at mixologists putting anything but a few drops of water (dripped from an eyedropper, of course) into their fine single malts, many are now embracing mustached bartenders shaking up their single malts with fresh juice, homemade tinctures, and spices. Even the distillery manager at LAPHROAIG was impressed by cocktails coming out of mixology meccas like San Francisco, New York, and London. Edinburgh is also home to a burgeoning cocktail scene, using their native spirits in creative concoctions. At Bramble Bar, an underground cocktail hub recognized as one of the top in the world, the bartender tossed me the house-bottled and aged Affinity Cocktail, a super-tasty and simple cocktail made with GLENMORANGIE 10 and vermouth and sealed and stamped with Bramble's own wax. The bar is one of the new forces bringing Scotch to the twenty-first century on its own playground.

Although not necessarily a spanking-new trend, distilleries are continuing to produce a spate of special-edition releases. Stories give whisky more meaning, and brands know that you're likely to remember a bottle that commemorates a piece of their history. ARDBEG released THE ROLLERCOASTER commemorating the ten-year anniversary of its fan club, BUNNAHABHAIN has a bottle to celebrate 125 years of making whisky, and GLENFIDDICH even debuted a special SNOW PHOENIX whisky commemorating the collapse of a warehouse roof during a heavy snowfall in 2010. CAOL ILA and LAGAVULIN put out special bottlings for the annual Islay Festival, and MACALLAN released a special edition for Prince William's wedding. Some distilleries are moving away from numbers and giving all sorts of names to their malts. THE DALMORE, for example, recently came out with a CIGAR MALT whisky—not that it has tobacco in it, but it's easier to remember than yet another number. Special bottlings are usually harder to find and come at a premium.

THE FUTURE

The Scotch industry has been marred with highs, lows, and international factors gnawing on its existence and then pushing it to new heights. Luckily, the graph is up and to the right and everything is growing faster than ever. The largest markets for Scotch consumption continue to be the United States and France (the French drink more Scotch than their own Cognac), though China, Taiwan, India, Singapore, and Brazil are not far behind. Brands are ramping up production and running stills 24-7 to supply whisky to millions of future consumers in emerging markets. **Since the Scotch made now won't be ready for close to a decade, brands are taking a hand at predicting the future and doubling down on future growth.** Sometimes world trends throw curveballs. The Greek economic crisis that changed the habits of a once-avid whisky-consuming nation is a good example. China's middle class is joining the market of whisky consumers and is already larger than the entire population of the United States. Fine Scotches are coveted in China as status symbols and many fakes are making their way into the market, which only pushes along the cultural demand. The most clever and poignant imitation I've seen is a "Johnnie Worker" Red Label, a spirit that is a quite a bit further than two letters from the genuine thing.

Women are also riding the new wave of Scotch. What was previously hailed as an old man's drink had a very sparse female history (though the CARDHU distillery was launched by Helen

Cumming). Old-fashioned prejudices and sexist hiring practices are withering away with more women running distilleries, becoming the face of brands, and stirring up cocktails with world fame. And it's about time. Women tend to have better palates and sense aroma more acutely. It's no surprise that having two X chromosomes actually makes women *superior* whisky tasters.

Like the thousand-year-old stone buildings along the cobblestone streets in Edinburgh, Scotch isn't changing anytime soon. It's deeply rooted in history and national pride and is more interwoven into Scottish culture than tartan. As whisky companies continue to grow exponentially, stylistic trends into the new millennium aren't likely to be drastic. Legal caution tape keeps flavors in check, and there is a scientific upper limit for how peaty a whisky can be. With shelves of single malts vying for your parched mouth, large marketing campaigns are going to become more creative, testing new ways to catch your eye. Consumers are getting wiser and want to know more about their whisky, who made it, and what to expect when they crack open the bottle. Brands will surely comply by adding more explicit descriptions and making their whisky more traceable.

The unicorn is a common symbol among Scottish cultural traditions. It's prancing on the national coat of arms and beckoning you to come drink from pools of the water of life. If you go out drinking tonight and forget everything in this chapter, remember that although Scotch sits high with regal aristocracy and has been a symbol of wealth and sophistication for hundreds of years, you should never take it too seriously. Like the one-horned mythical creature, fly high and let Scotch take you on epic adventures.

ROB ROY

The Scottish version of the Manhattan, this classic drink pays homage to a folk hero who is often said to be the Scottish Robin Hood. Born in the seventeenth century, he was a hero in his own time. The drink was first created at the Waldorf Hotel in New York in 1894.

1½ oz/45 ml Glenfiddich 12 single-malt whisky
½ oz/15 ml sweet vermouth
Dash of Angostura bitters
Ice cubes
1 lemon peel strip, for garnish

Combine the whisky, vermouth, and bitters in a mixing glass with ice cubes and stir until well chilled, about 15 seconds. Strain into a chilled cocktail glass and garnish with the lemon peel before serving.

BLOOD AND SAND

Named after a 1922 silent film that was based on a 1909 Spanish novel, this drink is a European original. Created from all European ingredients, the drink most likely grew in popularity around the time the United States was wading in Prohibition. Although the movie is a dark love triangle that ends with Rudolph Valentino getting gored in a bullfight, the drink is surprisingly delicious.

1½ oz/45 ml Johnnie Walker Black Label or other blended Scotch
1 oz/30 ml fresh orange juice
¾ oz/25 ml Cherry Heering or other cherry-flavored brandy
¾ oz/25 ml sweet vermouth
Ice cubes
1 brandied cherry, for garnish

Combine the Scotch, orange juice, brandy, and vermouth in a cocktail shaker with ice cubes and shake vigorously until well chilled, 20 to 30 seconds. Strain into a chilled cocktail glass and garnish with the brandied cherry before serving.

THE MANCHESTER

H. Joseph Ehrmann, San Francisco

This cocktail was originally made for a cocktail competition and was concocted mentally before H. even got to the liquor store. H. owns one of the oldest bars in San Francisco and is an icon in the cocktail industry. This is a beautifully herbaceous drink that is fairly easy to make if you have everything on hand.

Two 3-in/7.5-cm fresh rosemary sprigs

1¼ oz/40 ml Domaine de Canton ginger liqueur

1¼ oz/40 ml Glenmorangie 10 single-malt whisky

½ oz/15 ml Clover Honey Syrup (recipe follows)

½ oz/15 ml fresh lemon juice

1 large egg white

Ice cubes

Put the leaves from one rosemary sprig in the bottom of a cocktail shaker and bruise well with a muddler. Add the ginger liqueur, whisky, honey syrup, lemon juice, and egg white; cover; and shake vigorously for 5 seconds. Uncover, add ice, reseal, and shake well for 10 seconds more. Strain into a chilled coupe glass. Place the second rosemary sprig in the palm of one hand and slap it with the other hand. Garnish the drink with the rosemary before serving.

CLOVER HONEY SYRUP: In a jar, combine ½ cup/170 g clover honey and ½ cup/120 ml hot water and mix thoroughly. Pour into a squeeze bottle and store in the refrigerator. It will keep for 3 to 4 weeks.

THE ROYAL WARRANT

Jon Gasparini, San Francisco

As with all products that are issued royal warrants, this drink is fit for a king. The Earl Grey syrup and egg white help to mellow the peatiness of the whisky, and the tart citrus of the lemon juice helps to balance the drink. This cocktail is even garnished with bergamot orange (a cross between a Seville orange and a lemon or citron), one of the iconic aromas in Earl Grey tea. Jon knew what he was doing with this drink. He has started several successful bars in San Francisco, and this cocktail is a crowd-pleaser.

1½ oz/45 ml Lagavulin single-malt whisky
½ oz/15 ml Earl Grey Syrup (facing page)
½ oz/15 ml fresh lemon juice
½ organic egg white
2 dashes of orange bitters
Ice cubes
Bergamot orange, for garnish

Combine the whisky, Earl Grey syrup, lemon juice, egg white, and bitters in a cocktail shaker, cover, and shake vigorously for 20 to 30 seconds to emulsify the mixture. Uncover, add ice, reseal, and shake well for 15 seconds more. Strain into a chilled cocktail glass. Using a Microplane grater, garnish the drink with a little bergamot zest before serving.

EARL GREY SYRUP: In a saucepan, combine 1 cup/200 g organic sugar and 1 cup/240 ml water and bring to a boil, stirring to dissolve the sugar. Add 1 tbsp loose-leaf Earl Grey tea, reduce the heat, and simmer for 5 minutes, then remove from the heat and let cool completely. Strain into a sealable bottle, cap, and refrigerate until cold and viscous before using. The syrup will keep for up to 3 weeks.

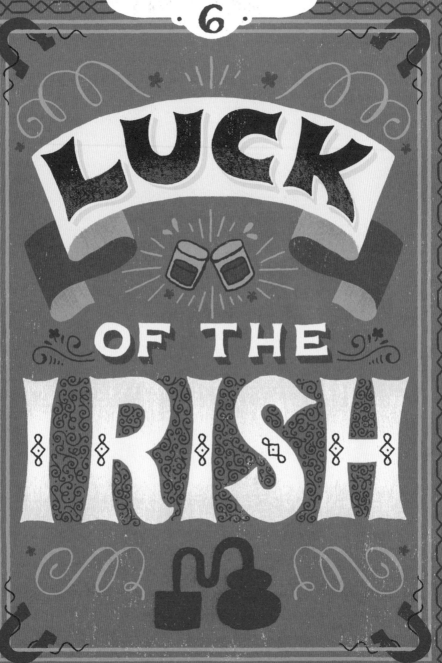

CHAPTER
· 6 ·

LUCK
OF THE
IRISH

Still hungover from the night before, I found myself wandering into the Brazen Head pub in Dublin. I made my way through the Euro-punk crew by the door and planted myself next to one of the regulars. Wrapped in a damp woolly sweater, he was gazing somewhere beyond the poster of a scantily clad promo model. This guy had been coming to the place longer than I've been alive, always sitting at the end of the bar and ordering the same drink: POWERS whiskey, overfilled rocks glass, neat, with a pint of Guinness. It was novel to sit with an old Irish bloke and sip on some whiskey that was first made just across the river from where we were sitting. It was astounding to find out that the bar we were sitting in was established in 1198, long before whiskey ever existed.

As luck would have it, whiskey was an Irish invention. In chapter 1, I described how the expertise of alcohol making crossed Europe. Monks saw these new distilled spirits as magical potions. What else could be used as an antiseptic, an anesthetic, and a total intoxicant all at the same time? Alchemists and religious leaders revered alcohol as the mystical water of life. The name "water of life" stuck quite literally, and *aqua vitae*, as it was called in Latin, became *uisce beatha* in Gaelic, which was then bastardized to *whiskey* in English. Although no longer so mysterious, whiskey continues to do magical things.

Irish whiskey used to be huge. The wee nation was the power-house of whiskey making from the mid-nineteenth into the early twentieth century. During those decades, Irish whiskey was found in bars around the world and in the bloodstream of drinkers from San Francisco to Tasmania. Drunken leprechauns poured free-flowing bottles, and pots of whiskey sat at the end of every rainbow. Its history was closely tied to the sociopolitical trends in both the United Kingdom and the United States, and although teetotal ramblings didn't push the country into prohibition, a perfect storm of unfortunate events effectively shriveled the industry to nil. Lucky for us, it's on its way back.

Coming out of World War I, where two hundred thousand Irish troops fought alongside the British forces, Ireland's atmosphere was wrought with nationalism. The year after the war ended, Ireland declared itself a sovereign republic that consequently launched into the Irish War of Independence. It was a three-year battle marked by guerilla violence and destruction in the major cities. Not only did the hostilities stunt the growth of the whiskey industry, but the new Irish nation also lost the international colonial markets and distribution networks of the vast British Commonwealth. Whiskey exports that stretched from Canada to South Africa, India to Australia were ripped away like petals off a shamrock. Although the Republic of Ireland was established in 1921, the following year was drenched in tensions that finally escalated into the Irish Civil War.

At the same time the fighting Irish were battling the Brits and then fighting themselves, America ratified the Eighteenth Amendment banning the manufacture and sale of all alcohol. As the United States was one of the largest importers of Irish whiskey, this was the final blow to the Irish whiskey industry. The bootleggers of the American underground came to Ireland for their whiskey fix, but not wanting to involve themselves in the American corruption machine, the Irish passed on the offer to export their whiskey. The chain of events shattered Irish whiskey and the industry was down for the count.

Only three major distilleries are still making whiskey on the island. Signs from old distilleries have been repurposed and built into part of Dublin's neighborhood decor. Although the whiskey scene was ripped apart in the first half of the 1900s, renewed world interest in the spirit is breathing new life into the industry that might also be a partial answer to Ireland's economic issues. Glasses of whiskey aren't just drowning economic sorrows, they're growing the country's exports, increasing the workforce, and making Irish culture a hot commodity once again. **Ireland still sits behind Japan in global whiskey production, but gears are greased and the Irish whiskey clover might just be growing a fourth leaf.**

CELTIC STYLE

Because the Scots learned how to make whiskey from the Irish, the whiskies are similar, made in almost identical ways and presenting tastes that mimic each other. The technical differences are small ones, and although they do affect the taste, they are not strict rules. The three major operating distilleries make a broad range of whiskies to satisfy any palate.

The first thing that most Irishmen will explain (after pointing out the spelling) is that Irish whiskey is distilled three times. It sets it apart from other whiskies and makes the spirit lighter bodied. Think about vodka brands that boast triple, quadruple, or even a hundred-times distillation. They're explaining how pure their spirit is (and in the case of vodka, that it has even less taste). Distilling Irish whiskey a third time makes it smoother and takes out some of the impurities that add bolder tastes and can give you bigger headaches. The reality is that not all Irish whiskey is distilled thrice, and there are Scotches (like AUCHENTOSHAN) that are put through the still three times. Keep an eye out for the details that the distillery puts on the label.

The second generalization to know about Irish whiskey is that it's not peated. Most Irish whiskies lack that earthy, smoky flavor you find in Scotch because barley in Ireland is malted with natural gas or hot air. However, peat was surely used centuries ago when the industry first started, and a couple of whiskies are still made with smoked barley.

Ireland has its single malts that come from one distillery and blends that use grain spirits in the mix. It also has its own third category of pure pot still whiskies, sometimes called single pot still. These whiskies aren't blends, but they aren't single malts either. Accordingly to the big book of rules, to be single malt, a whiskey has to be made entirely from malted barley and come from only one distillery. This third category of pure pot still whiskies uses both malted barley and unmalted, or green, barley and is made at a single distillery. It's a trend that started when the British government decided to tax malted barley in 1802. At the time, Irish whiskey was the biggest exported whiskey in the world, and the British government wanted a cut. The Irish distillers were clever and sidestepped the tax collectors by using a mix of malted and unmalted barley to lower their costs. The resulting mix created a style that continues to shape the flavor and identity of Irish whiskey. It's a subtle categorical difference, a very small shift in the ingredients, but it can cause big changes, bringing grassier flavors to the mix. Even JAMESON, one of the country's major distillers, still uses unmalted barley, but since all of its styles are blends, they aren't pure pot still whiskies. The two most common and classic pure pot still whiskies are GREEN SPOT and REDBREAST, both full-bodied, full-flavored whiskies that have won several awards but are still not distributed widely.

NAMING NAMES

The two giants of the Irish whiskey world are BUSHMILLS in Northern Ireland and JAMESON (which was once made in the center of Dublin) in the south. BUSHMILLS is one of the oldest licensed distilleries in the world, with a permit to distill in the area granted by James I in 1608. The distillery bottles its flagship brand, a premium blend, and a series of different aged single malts. **BUSHMILLS ORIGINAL** is its most popular blend and is a great whiskey for a mixed drink (try it with lemonade). The manager of the distillery said his grandfather would always shout "Gimme a Bush" to his bartenders when he wanted the premium **BLACK BUSH** blend, and he would hold on to the 16-year-old single malt as a special treat when his kids were home for Christmas. **BUSHMILLS** is fairly transparent about the casks they use in their single malts, and it's a great way to taste your way through whiskies that have aged in varying barrels. The 10-year-old is finished in mostly sherry casks (you can see it in the darker color), and the 16-year-old is aged in a mix of old bourbon, sherry, and port casks. I've been told that a lot of one-time **FOUR ROSES** casks are used, so you may even taste a hint of Kentucky pride in the single malts.

Both Scotland and Ireland have a long history of using sherry barrels. In 1588, the Spanish Armada tried to invade Britain in order to overthrow Elizabeth I. It's said that after dozens of ships were wrecked off the coast of Ireland, the Irish found sherry barrels and commandeered them for whiskey making. Soon after the Spanish fleet's failed attempt, written records make mention of the first Irish whiskey aged in sherry casks. It was the start of a long and tasty relationship. To this day, **BUSHMILLS** distillery sits on the stunning Northern Ireland coast, just a short galleon ride from the Scottish islands.

JAMESON, the second whiskey giant, is the quintessential Irish staple in every bar (even though, like St. Patrick, John Jameson was Scottish to the core). John Jameson moved to Ireland with dreams of making whiskey during Dublin's equivalent of the dot-com boom. He worked at one of the hundreds of budding distilleries and was later able to purchase the company and slap his name on the brand. **JOHN JAMESON & SON** grew with unbridled success to become one of the world's largest-selling whiskies. Since the 1800s, it has been sold internationally, and it was the whiskey I studied on Saturday nights in college. As the flagship brand of the company, it helped define Irish whiskey worldwide. You've had it with friends at the local bar, and there are specials on it every March 17. It's not the fanciest whiskey in the world, but it's light and approachable. It's perfect for mixing, for taking a series of shots, and for a night of heavy drinking.

Most people don't realize that **JAMESON** also makes an entire line of reserve whiskies, with a wide range of qualities and prices. These higher-end blends are making their way into the bar where previously there was room for only one bottle of **JAMESON**. All **JAMESON** whiskies are blends, made with different ratios of single pot still whiskey to light base spirits. The older the age, the more expensive the bottle and the more pot still whiskey in the recipe. Each and every bottle of Jameson has the Latin words *sine metu* printed on the label. Latin for "without fear," the family motto is said to be from the days of fighting pirates.

Although **JAMESON** and **BUSHMILLS** are popular throughout Ireland, the country has its own major blends that occupy space behind every domestic bar. With histories similar to **JAMESON**, **POWERS** and **PADDY** hold the number-one and number-three spots, respectively, as the bestselling whiskies in Ireland. Both were among the first companies to bottle their whiskies (previously all whiskey was sold in ceramic casks), and like **TULLAMORE DEW**, both are currently made at the same distillery that produces **JAMESON**. More and more often, you can also find them at bars in the United States.

The other major distillery is **COOLEY** (owned by Diageo), located north of Dublin. It makes a few flagship brands, such as **GREENORE** and **TYRCONNELL**, and a few peated whiskies, including **CONNEMARA**. Some of the newest Irish whiskey is being made at the oldest distillery in the world. Due east of Dublin, **KILBEGGAN** distillery was established in 1757 and still has the old wooden gears, antique tanks, and an early waterwheel that can power the entire operation. It had been out of commission for half a century, but the small stills are being fired up and its whiskey is not far behind.

Whiskey doesn't have a religion. The common rumor is that **JAMESON** and **BUSHMILLS** are archnemeses because one is in historically Protestant Northern Ireland and the other is in the Catholic south. Although they may both be competing for your mouth and money, the competition between them is not a religious one. John Jameson was actually a Scottish Protestant, and the regional fable has been mostly fueled by Irish Americans. Although the two Irelands have endured a difficult history of fighting and terrorism, many Irishmen would be happy to come together and have a drink. Just don't order an Irish Car Bomb.

DRINKING LIKE THE IRISH

The Irish drink a lot. From my experience, they drink copious amounts more than the Scottish. Irish pubs stay open until the wee hours, and it's not uncommon to see folks stumbling home around four o'clock in the morning. Two of the top touristic sites in Ireland are the Guinness brewery and the old **JAMESON** distillery, and as you know, Irish pubs are so famous that they've planted themselves in every major city around the world. And there is a reason for that. In Ireland, blood doesn't just flow green; it flows with a stench of booze. The classic old-timer's drink is a shot of whiskey with a Guinness on the side. There is tremendous national pride in Ireland, and anything Irish is inherently superior to its Scottish counterpart. As the Irish story has it, the Scots dropped the *e* in whiskey because they're lazy.

In an area called Temple Bar, Dublin's epicenter of young drunken tourism, there's a bar aptly named Temple Bar that has made itself the face of the neighborhood. The pub is decked out with **JAMESON**, **BUSHMILLS**, **POWERS**, and Guinness paraphernalia, and it has an oversized statue of a man standing on a barrel, whiskey in hand. It's a statue to the unknown whiskey drinker, a legendary man who would come in during pivotal moments in history, drink a ton of Irish whiskey, and stand on a barrel to recite poetry. More symbolic than it is historical, it's a reminder that Ireland's history and its whiskey go hand in hand. Outside of this bar, I met a tattooed window washer wearing a newsboy hat who knew more about Irish whiskey than Wikipedia did. To his delight, we chatted for a good thirty minutes about esoteric Irish whiskey history and forgotten brands. He is part of this whiskey generation that isn't just about getting sloshed and starting bar fights. He's the reason Irish whiskey never completely died.

———

Despite its rocky history, Irish whiskey is here to stay. Several more brands have showed up on the market in recent years, and the world is looking for alternatives to green beer on St. Patrick's Day. **We're at a pinnacle where we can use the words *Irish* and *whiskey* together in the same sentence without having to head to Shenanigans Irish pub for Celtic folk songs and corned beef.** Whiskey brands are seeing record sales, and haphazard endorsements from Lady Gaga (and her infatuation with her boyfriend "Jameson") to Rihanna haven't hurt the trend. As some of the bigger brands are making premium bottles and pure pot still whiskies are making their rounds into new markets, whiskey drinkers and media are realizing that Ireland has picked up where it left off. Ireland is firing its stills with the enthusiasm that hasn't been seen since the turn of the century. After all, the island that invented whiskey must have something to show for itself six hundred years later.

IRISH COFFEE

The history of Irish coffee is decidedly Irish, but it lands Stateside in a particular bar in San Francisco. Whiskey was commonly served in tea throughout Ireland, but pouring it into coffee was unusual. A server at a café at the flying-boat station in Foynes, Ireland, was the first to serve what we know today as Irish coffee. The drink became well known at the Shannon Airport and travelers caught wind of it. The recipe was debated and re-created at the Buena Vista café in San Francisco and popularized among Americans. To this day, the Buena Vista serves thousands of Irish coffees to tourists from around the world. The key to the drink is really fresh cream.

6 oz/180 ml freshly brewed hot coffee
1½ oz/45 ml Jameson or other Irish whiskey
1 tsp brown sugar
About 2 tbsp softly whipped cream

In a mug, combine the coffee, whiskey, and brown sugar and stir to dissolve the sugar. Hold a teaspoon upside down over the coffee mixture and gently pour the whipped cream onto the spoon, allowing it to flow gently onto the surface of the coffee. Using the spoon will help the cream to remain floating on the surface. Do not stir. Serve hot.

SIDESHOW

Shaher Misif, San Francisco

Most people's introduction to whiskey cocktails is through the classics. This recipe, from an award-winning San Francisco mixologist, presents a new way to dive into the spirit. It's simple to make at home and a balanced mix of flavors.

2 oz/60 ml Bushmills Original whiskey
½ oz/15 ml fresh grapefruit juice
½ oz/15 ml fresh lime juice
½ oz/15 ml Clover Honey Syrup (see page 113)
Dash of Angostura bitters
Ice cubes
Sparkling wine, to finish

Combine the whiskey, grapefruit juice, lime juice, honey syrup, and bitters in a cocktail shaker with ice and shake vigorously until well chilled, 20 to 30 seconds. Strain into a flute and top off with the sparkling wine before serving.

I THINK I'M TURNING JAPANESE

If you've seen Sofia Coppola's *Lost in Translation*, it taught you two major things: Bill Murray's lack of enthusiasm can drive you to drink enough for three, and Japan has a compulsive obsession with whisky. I wouldn't be the least bit surprised if the movie was your first introduction to the fact that Japanese whisky exists. It isn't a completely different spirit from what you know. It's not going to smell like sushi or impart a burning wasabi sensation. Because the barley and most of the handmade copper stills are imported from Europe, its taste will fall in line with whisky made in the Scottish tradition. It is produced and served with subtle Japanese nuances that may be lost to a first- or second-time drinker. I've seen blog posts and comments from enthusiasts who don't quite understand why Japanese whiskies would ever be marketed *without* a famous face like Bill Murray's on the advertisement. But as you'll discover, there is more to Japanese whisky than the aging Irish American actor.

Too many of your friends probably still think Japanese whisky is a joke. They think it's the equivalent of vodka made in Mexico or wine from Inner Mongolia. A good friend of mine who was in Tokyo during 9/11 told me he reached for a bottle of Japanese whisky assuming it would give him a vicious enough hangover to forget the day before. Needless to say, some Japanese whisky is rotgut. There are Mexican tequilas, Polish vodkas, and, dare I say, French Champagnes that are total crap. It may take a few minutes to learn which bottles of Japanese whisky to try, and a few more yen to appreciate them.

WHY JAPAN?

To understand Japanese whisky, you first have to develop an understanding of Scotch. That's because Japanese whisky was not a product of its environment. Instead, it was born out of an insatiable desire to drink the best in the world. Whisky was embraced as a hot Western commodity, and economic and cultural circumstances drove Japanese demand for a homegrown alternative to expensive and lesser-known Scotches. The Japanese have a natural aptitude for taking someone else's invention, learning it, and then perfecting it so it is their own. Sushi originated on mainland Asia and eventually moved to Japan, where it changed from cured fish to raw fish and was honed into the culinary art that it is today (that is, until it was bastardized in order to fill grocery-store refrigerators in California with fake crab rolls). Although Nikons and Canons are the name brands at the forefront of world photography, Japan was also half a century behind the development of the camera in France in the early 1800s and the onslaught of personal cameras developed by James Eastman and his Kodak Company in the United States in the early twentieth century. When made-in-Japan cameras flashed on the world stage, they became known as the world's best. Japanese distillers have successfully done the same with whisky.

It would be difficult for the nonexpert to decipher differences in taste between Japanese whisky and Scotch. **I'm not going to try to sum up tens of thousands of years of Japanese culture into a few sentences, but a purity and attention to detail shine through in Japanese whisky making.** I can't capture the essence of a perfect piece of *maguro nigiri* sushi by telling you that it's a chunk of tuna on a pad of rice. If you traced that one piece back to its origin, you would discover volumes on Japanese fishing habits, treatises on the flash freezing of tuna at sea, and observations on how the traditions of auctioning fish at Tokyo's Tsukiji fish market play into the whole equation, not to mention how years of training by the sushi chef go into preparing a perfect *nigiri*. In the same way, Japanese tradition has shaped the development and production of whisky. Whereas American bourbon was an invention of regional necessity, Japanese distillers have studied age-old Scottish traditions and have designed a classic product with fresh eyes.

With few exceptions, water is one of the only Japanese ingredients in most Japanese whisky. Since water makes up the bulk of any whisky, it's key to the recipe, and many of Japan's distilleries have been built close to fantastic water sources. The **HAKUSHU** distillery, on Honshu, Japan's main island, even bottles and sells the water that is used for its whisky. For the most part, broad generalizations about Japanese whisky are difficult. It is made in the same manner as it is everywhere else in the world: aged in used oak barrels that previously held bourbon, sherry, or other wines. Several Japanese distilleries age some of their whisky in casks made from Japanese oak (*mizunara*). Differences in taste are subtle, but the domestic wood can bring out flavors of coconut, sandalwood, and spice. Other distilleries are experimenting with local peat from the northern island of Hokkaido, and with locally grown barley, which can give whisky fruitier flavors.

Whisky in Japan is no small business. In fact, Japan has moved its way up the charts to become the third-largest whisky-producing nation in the world, trailing only the United Kingdom and the United States. Its brief history has already made legends, and its fame has shot into the limelight faster than a bullet train. Japanese whisky doesn't have the centuries-old lore and ancient cultural traditions that sake has, but keen production and attention to quality have quickly expedited its development into an extremely successful twentieth-century sprint. We are in the midst of history in the making, but it didn't start off with such greatness.

THE HISTORY

Rewind to the hazy beginnings of Japanese whisky history. Shrouded in stories painted by large corporate public relations departments and a drunken blur, whisky in Japan has no clear start. The "official" beginning is usually put at 1923, but an interesting lineage of liquor lore exists. Before World War I, way back before you were pounding down sake bombs and picking up rainbow rolls at the grocery store, Japan was an isolated country with few connections to the Western world. Handfuls of outsiders made it to Japan, and some undoubtedly carried bottles of Scotch with them to keep warm. The smuggled whisky must have whetted palates and sparked ingenuity among chemists and barkeeps. As the story goes, a gaggle of American soldiers stopped in a northern Japanese port in 1918 and tried a Japanese "Scotch" called Queen George. The adventure ends with a drunken rambling brigade and the world's first documented story of a Japanese whisky tasting.

The chemists that created the first domestic whiskies weren't trying to make a Japanese product. They were trying to pass off cheap bottles of flavored alcohol labeled "Scotch whisky" to fill an interest in Western goods. It was likely nauseating, but luckily for the soldiers, it still got them drunk. Queen George, like other so-called whiskies that were being made in Japan, struck a chord of curiosity and sparked domestic interest in a spirit that would soon be the heart of a new Japanese industry.

As more international influences crept onto the island nation after the Great War, Japan became accustomed to some of the finer ways of Western life, including whisky. Japan already had a host of breweries making sake and distilleries creating other spirits, namely *shōchū,* the distinctly Japanese alcohol that can be fashioned from one of several ingredients, including barley (*mugi shōchū*). Although *shōchū* doesn't taste much like whisky, the equipment and distillation expertise made the jump to whisky an easier one. A couple of ambitious Japanese entrepreneurs and avid whisky enthusiasts decided that instead of importing all of their Scotch, it was time for Japan to take a seat on the world whisky stage and make it in their own backyard.

One of these entrepreneurs, Masataka Taketsuru, took things to the next level. Born into a family of sake brewers, he learned to appreciate alcohol at a young age and became infatuated with whisky—so much so that shortly after the end of World War I, he was chosen by his boss to travel halfway across the world to Scotland to learn the trade. He signed up for chemistry courses at the University of Glasgow and then headed to the distilleries. He landed a couple of apprenticeships and took countless notes on the ins and outs of whisky making. He was only twenty-five at the time, yet these were just the first steps for the Godfather of Japanese Whisky. It was this journey and the knowledge that he brought back to Japan that led to the development of a Japanese whisky industry in the Scottish style. If instead, Taketsuru had enrolled in a university Stateside and wandered around the bourbon distilleries of the American South, Japanese whisky would have grown in a completely different direction—particularly because he would have landed just before Prohibition was kicking into gear.

Taketsuru returned to Japan with keen distilling and blending expertise, along with meticulous handwritten notes and a new Scottish wife. He linked up with Shinjiro Torii, a businessman who had started his own alcohol import company. A few years later, they started YAMAZAKI distillery, with Taketsuru as the manager. The company, initially called KOTOBUKIYA, was the precursor to today's Suntory corporation, a brand that was a combination of an alternative spelling to Torii's own name and the word *sun*. The significance of the word *sun*? Look no further than the Japanese flag and the country's nickname, Land of the Rising Sun. Long before the company took the Suntory name in 1963, Taketsuru had some fundamental disagreements with Torii and split off to start what is now the NIKKA distillery, on Hokkaido. He wanted to create a whisky in a more Scottish style, and Hokkaido presented a climate most similar to the regions where he learned the trade.

BUDDING INDUSTRY

To kick-start the trade, Japanese distilleries began by copying Scotland grain for grain. With the Japanese focus on precision, several distillers went so far as to dent their own stills where they noticed dents in the Scottish originals. Despite these initial attempts by Japanese chemists and distillers to replicate a royal Scottish spirit, Japanese whisky has come into its own. When judged in international competitions, Japanese whiskies are pitted against some of the world's finest Scotches and have begun to claim top awards. **In a flavor comparison, it's easiest to understand Japanese whisky as a new region in an alternate universe of Scotland.** Most winos wouldn't say that California wines are cheap copies of French and Italian masterpieces. Nor is modern Japanese whisky simply a Xerox of Scottish spirits. In very Japanese style, distillers and chemists have pulled apart the whisky-making guessing game and honed in on manipulating and creating their target flavors.

Japan's whisky industry has come out of puberty. Its malts increased dramatically in quality over the latter part of the twentieth century, and will undoubtedly gain notoriety and fame into this century. It continues to be a great sense of pride for the country and a liquid ambassador for Japanese culture. The first internationally acclaimed award came in 2001, when *Whisky*

Magazine named **NIKKA YOICHI** 10-year-old the Best of the Best. That recognition, as well as several other recent honors, helped transform Japan into a viable whisky nation.

JAPANESE DRINKING JAPANESE

Just as Japanese whisky was not a well-known spirit until recent years, the spirit took a while to catch on in the Japanese drinking scene. The first imported Scotches were big peaty monoliths that didn't sit well with Japanese taste. After all, Japanese food is light and alcohol traditions (think sake) reflect subtle and much gentler spirits. A heavy, smoky, and peated whisky would surely do a great job desensitizing your mouth for a delicate piece of salmon sashimi. However, drinking culture in Japan is bigger than Godzilla, and it didn't take long for hordes of consumers and Japanese salarymen to take a liking to whisky. As postwar Japan became more integrated into the rest of the world, foreign imports began to flow. To meet domestic demand and take a slice of the market, Japan started producing whisky in homegrown distilleries. After the destruction from the war, Japanese companies had to grow in creative ways. Suntory pushed their cheaper whiskies under the name **TORYS**, with the slogan "It's good, it's cheap." Several years later, the cartoon character Uncle Torys came to television, magazines, and posters around Japan. He was a crude drawing of a round white man with a pointy nose who frolicked on drinking adventures. He even turned red in the face after drinking, illustrating to a new market of consumers that the Asian glow, also known as the alcohol flush reaction, is a normal phenomenon. It was all marketing in the name of getting Japanese consumers to drink more whisky. Many of the new Japanese distilleries struggled to compete with cheap imports and could not compare to the quality from brands that had hundreds of years of practice on their side. As these newborn brands made it through the following decades, they focused on their domestic market.

The marketing of Japanese whisky paid off, and helped fuel a domestic mania for the stuff. The eccentric advertising continued into the 1970s, 1980s, and 1990s, even getting Sean Connery to be the face of Suntory's questionable CREST whisky in a 1992 commercial. I can only imagine the reaction of Scotch distillers who saw the Scottish actor as a face of the curious Japanese brand. It would have been the equivalent of Nicolas Sarkozy starring in a commercial for American cheese.

DRINKING, JAPANESE STYLE

Only a handful of Japanese whiskies make it to liquor shops and bars in the United States, though new products are landing every year. Today's whisky culture in Japan is growing, but it is marked by stark differences from elsewhere in the world. On the one side is a new generation of whisky drinkers who are integrating the spirit into nightlife and casual drinking. On the other end are whisky fanatics and specialty bars that have made whisky an obsession. Bars either have a handful of Scotches and common Japanese whiskies, or they have a twenty-page bible of their collection. Some bars have shelves of rare bottles from Scotland, and a handful focus solely on obscure Japanese whiskies.

THE CALCULATED RISE OF THE HIGHBALL

In a very intentional marketing push from whisky giant Suntory, drinkers are ordering highballs at nearly every watering hole in Japan. They are perhaps the easiest of mixed drinks to make, and in Japan are the equivalent of a Scotch and soda. To make one at home, it's a bit of whisky with a bunch of soda water. **Highballs are a logical and refreshing replacement for beer and are helping boost a whisky industry that has seen years of decline.** Suntory's marketing campaign hit big among a younger population who needed a light and simple drink to help them ease into whisky. When I sat down for a tasting at the beautifully sited HAKUSHU distillery, I asked my guide how she drinks her single malts. Without hesitating, she giggled, "Highball," as if I should have already known.

There are bars in Tokyo dedicated to highballs and many others that serve highballs on tap. As they generally contain two to three times as much soda as whisky, highballs are a simple way to curb your liquor and enjoy a light tipple on a hot summer evening. You can even walk into almost any corner store (it's legal to drink on the streets in Tokyo) and pick up a cold canned premixed highball on your way out—just like a soda.

CREATIVE MIXOLOGY

Other bars in Japan are getting more creative with whisky, and Japanese mixologists are experimenting with the spirit, pouring whisky over hand-carved ice spheres and serving some of the most amazing and rare spirits in the world. While walking down a snaking alley near Shibuya in central Tokyo, I popped my head into a bar with a sign outside that just read Bar. Like many bars in Tokyo, it was a complete Alice in Wonderland transformation from the bustle of the city to a dark, quiet, candle-lit rectangular room with seating for eight. The bartender was also the owner, janitor, bar back, host, and security. Using the little Japanese I knew, I asked for a cocktail of his choosing. My only request was that it be made with Japanese whisky. He grabbed an Asian pear (just known as pears in Japan), blended it with some YAMAZAKI 12, and delivered it in a beautiful presentation. It was made with the utmost care and was an incredible balance of sweet, fresh, and savory—a clean, surprisingly simple, and delicious cocktail. Here is my re-creation of that memorable drink, along with the name I coined for it.

PEAR AND SIMPLE

2 oz/60 ml Yamazaki 12
¼ Asian pear, peeled and cored
2 small ice cubes

Combine the whisky, pear, and ice cubes in a blender and process until smooth, about 30 seconds. Strain into a chilled cocktail glass to serve.

REGIONALITY

Regionality in Japan is defined by individual distilleries. The handful of distilleries that exist were built in several key areas for strategic reasons, including weather, convenience for shipping, and nearby water sources. Differences in the taste shine through variance in climate and their unique water supply. For example, YAMAZAKI's hard water leaves a unique footprint on its whisky, and the soft water at HAKUSHU imparts a softer, lighter taste.

Relationships of the companies in Japan affect the manner in which whiskies are made, mixed, and blended. Of the working distilleries in the country, five are owned by the trio of large alcohol companies, Suntory, NIKKA (owned by Asahi), and KIRIN.

Whereas Scottish distilleries often send barrels off to blending houses, independent bottling companies, and even other distilleries, Japanese whisky makers rarely trade whisky. A Scotch blend might have whisky from more than forty different distilleries, while Japanese blends will rarely mix more than two or three whiskies. Because of this, Japanese distilleries have set out to make a much broader range of styles that can be mixed together in-house. A single malt from one distillery, then, could have a much wider range of flavors than a similar product in Scotland. It's virtually impossible to say that a single distillery makes whisky in any one particular style.

There are fewer than a dozen operating whisky distilleries in Japan, but rather than list each and every one, here is a small sampling menu for your tasting pleasure. A few brands own more than one distillery, so keep in mind that the name of the whisky is not necessarily the name of the distillery. For example, NIKKA owns two Japanese distilleries of different names, as well as BEN NEVIS distillery in Scotland. The NIKKA whiskies can come from either of the distilleries, a blend of both, or even have BEN NEVIS single malt in the mix. If you really want to dive into Japanese whisky, do as the Japanese do and learn the nuanced historical trends and species of trees around each distillery. If nothing else, spend a couple of minutes learning the names of a few distilleries. Unless you're in the mother country, chances are you'll need to order them by name, and the knowledge will be your treasure map to Japanese pearls.

Suntory

Established by Shinjiro Torii in 1923, YAMAZAKI is the flagship whisky distillery of the Suntory corporation and of Japan. It is one of the largest distilleries in the world and makes the best-known and most widely available Japanese single malt, namely,

YAMAZAKI 12. This is the bottle that you are most likely to see behind the bar and in cocktails. The location for the distillery was heavily debated, but it was finally set up in an area with moderate weather, a nearby fresh water supply, and proximity to two large Japanese cities, Kyoto and Osaka. The distillery has six large stills and makes more than fifty styles of whisky that are subsequently bottled as single malts and mixed into blends several ways. In case a square watermelon the price of an iPhone isn't fancy enough to get for your boss, YAMAZAKI has offered a rare 50-year-old single malt for the cost of a small car (1,000,000 yen).

YAMAZAKI is an icon throughout Japan and on the international whisky scene. It has won a tremendous number of awards and notoriety for consistently tasty whisky. The master blender at YAMAZAKI tastes more than three hundred whisky samples each day, and to keep his palate consistent, every day he eats only *udon* for lunch. He is a whisky samurai, and his work is not just a job; it's a way of life.

If you head to the HAKUSHU distillery, you hurl toward Mount Fuji at 186 miles per hour (300 kilometers per hour to be authentic about it). The train slows down as it passes dense forests and a few small towns and approaches the town of Hakushu. The distillery was at one point the world's largest. The air is fresh and crisp, and the cool temperature slows down the aging of the whisky. The entire area is filled with lush green trees and is a beautiful setting to enjoy a dram and listen to the birds.

HAKUSHU makes whiskies that range from a 10-year-old, which is clean and light, to an 18-year-old, with more complexity and smoke. It even makes a "heavily peated" single malt that approaches the intensity and full body of Islay Scotch. These whiskies are just starting to make their way into the international market.

Suntory makes single malts and a range of blends at both YAMAZAKI and HAKUSHU. Like most whisky giants, it churns out massive quantities of cheaper booze to satiate drunken Japanese hipsters and salarymen passed out on the train-station steps. The company's standard blend comes in a famous turtle-shell glass bottle with a yellow label. On the higher end of the scale, Suntory makes its beautiful HIBIKI blend (Japanese for "balance" or "resonance"). The glass bottle is a stunning piece of artwork itself, with twenty-four facets that represent the twenty-four Japanese seasons. Each of the four expressions of the brand has won awards around the world, starting in 2004. That just so happens to be the year after the iconic HIBIKI bottle found its way in front of a movie camera in Bill Murray's hands.

Nikka

Soon after Taketsuru, the Godfather of Japanese Whisky, split off from the YAMAZAKI distillery, he headed north to the island of Hokkaido to start what is now called the YOICHI distillery (the name of which coincidentally means "first son"), owned by the NIKKA alcohol company. It was the location where he had originally wanted to build YAMAZAKI because of the area's cooler weather. The distillery has been in operation since 1936 and introduced its first bottle four years later. One of the notable things about YOICHI is that the distillery still uses coal to heat its stills. It's an antiquated practice that Taketsuru learned in Scotland, though nowadays few Scotch distilleries continue to use coal.

NIKKA's other distillery, MIYAGIKYO, is in Sendai, on Japan's main island, not far from the epicenter of the devastating earthquake and tsunami of 2011. Fortunately, the distillery was not heavily damaged and it is still a whisky powerhouse in the region. Like Suntory, NIKKA makes all sorts of whiskies. One of the most common and most consumed is the lower-end **BLACK NIKKA**, a cheap blend branded with a bearded, blue-eyed Scotsman whose likeness is that of the original Scottish whisky blender. **NIKKA** also bottles some beautiful single malts from its two distilleries. Many of the whiskies from **YOICHI** follow the heavier, smokier trends of Scotches. As noted earlier, it was one of **YOICHI**'s single malts that won Japan's first international whisky award.

Kirin

Yet another big name in the Japanese alcohol scene, **KIRIN** (think Kirin beer) has owned two whisky distilleries. **FUJI-GOTEMBA** sits near the foot of Mount Fuji and uses water that was once ice at the top of the mountain's triangular peak. If you come across a whisky that says Fuji anywhere on the label, most likely it was made near the highest mountain in Japan. The other distillery, **KARUIZAWA**, is no longer in use but was famous for producing heavy, oaky, peated whiskies. Bottles from these distilleries are not easy to find abroad and are best sought in specialty shops. The name Kirin is an alternative spelling of Qilin, the Chinese fire-breathing monster that shows up during the arrival of wise sages. The next time you're drinking **KIRIN** whisky, make sure to pair it with an inspiring TED talk.

Chichibu

Nestled in the hills north of Tokyo, **CHICHIBU** is Japan's newest distillery. Set up in 2007 and the first distillery to be built in Japan since the 1970s, it is owned and operated by whisky pioneer Ichiro Akuto. After my taxi driver mistakenly drove to three bars and a sake brewery, I mumbled Ichiro's name and he finally understood where I wanted to go. Every drop of whisky bottled at the distillery passes by Ichiro's inspection, and all blending first happens in his mouth. Although his brand, ICHIRO'S MALT, is relatively new, Ichiro's grandfather started the HANYU distillery (no longer in use) in 1946, and his family has been in the alcohol industry for generations.

Ichiro's family didn't start learning the Scottish way of making whisky until the 1980s. He doesn't always eat *udon* for lunch, but he did chuckle when I inquired and said that maybe one day he'll get there. He is still inventing and constantly developing new products, inspired by the many other whiskies he tries. Aside from having a creative playing-card motif, most of his hand-labeled bottles are marked with each whisky's detailed résumé. Perusing the distillery's malts is a great exercise in tasting and understanding subtle differences among whiskies. One of the bottles I tried was a single malt newborn double-matured whisky. Without any details, I'd be pretty confused as to what I was drinking, but the label carried all of this information:

DISTILLERY: Chichibu	**CASK TYPE**: 1st Bourbon Barrel, 2nd New American Oak
DISTILLED: April—May 2008	
1ST CASK IN: May—June 2008	**VARIETY OF BARLEY**: Braemar Non-Peated
2ND CASK IN: June 2009	
BOTTLED: Nov 2009	**BATCH SIZE**: 400kg of Malt
ALCOHOL BY VOLUME: 61.4 percent	**WASH BACK**: 4no. 3100L "Mizunara" Wood
VOLUME: 700 ml	
CASK#: 445	**POT STILLS**: 2no. 2000L Copper Straight Head, Downward Line Arm, Indirect Fire, Shell, and tube condenser
CHILL FILTRATION: No	
ARTIFICIAL COLOR: No	

This is more information than you could ever ask for on a whisky bottle. It is essentially the distiller's notes to himself and the rec-ipe to make this particular bottle. Knowing these kinds of details is invaluable and can enable you to taste the subtle differences in the way a whisky is made. Although pieces of this information are available for some whiskies online, the full genetic makeup is usually far from view.

Chichibu is small, with a Shinto shrine on the wall, and built with incredible attention to detail. The tasting room, with its shelves of single malts and blends, looks like a chemistry lab. The distillery's output is for a niche market and is poured by high-end bartenders, a few American connoisseurs, and Japanese whisky aficionados. Since the demand for Ichiro's whisky far exceeds his production, and he's already winning awards, he's bound to grow in the coming years. In many ways, he is the living history of a new chapter of fine Japanese whiskies.

INTO YOUR MOUTH

A very small percentage of whiskies from Japan make their way onto the mainstream consumer highway. The ones that do cost a pretty penny. Thanks to vocal tourists and expats in Japan, plus a stockpile of blogs, it's getting easier to learn about Japanese whisky and stay on top of news coming out of a country that all too often keeps information in its native tongue.

Obviously, the best way to understand Japanese whisky is to go to Japan and head to the distilleries. After you've done that, wander the streets and try to follow directions to the absolutely insane Japanese bars—no, not Tokyo's obscure prison-, Jesus-, or Mario Brothers—themed venues, but the bars lined with walls of local whiskies. Stumbling into a local liquor store will be an adult's FAO Schwarz dream. **Tokyo has more Michelin-starred restaurants than any city in the world, and it has built a tour de force of whisky to match.** Don't worry if your Japanese isn't perfect and you can read only two out of the three alphabets used to write Japanese: whisky in Japanese is just called *uisukī*. If you're not on your way to Tokyo, the easiest entry into Japan's collection will be a dram of YAMAZAKI 12 single malt or a HIBIKI blend. They are the most common around the world and set a high benchmark for quality Japanese whisky.

The Japanese whisky industry has grown into maturity twice as fast as other major whisky players. It's clear that both the large established companies and the niche independent brands are viable competition in worldwide tastings. Japanese whiskies have just begun their foray into winning awards and will slowly trickle into more international markets and local bars.

As some of the newer distilleries mature, future generations are going to take note of what happened during the shift of the spirit in the beginning of the twenty-first century. The trend is creating a new wave of Japanophiles who are obsessed with more than anime and Hello Kitty. Preconceived notions and haunting images of Bill Murray are finally shattering. On the ground in Tokyo, the army of highballs will lead some to an interest in single malts and Western-style cocktails. It's already common to find bartenders who are studying and mastering whisky in ways that would spin heads around the world. Japan has shown the world that its whisky is worthy of attention, and now the marketing geniuses behind the brands are in the process of convincing a new Japanese generation that they should ditch their gothic Lolita Harajuku costumes and *kanpai* (toast) to a single malt. It's going to be difficult to shake off the memories of domestic whisky from the 1980s, an era that was searching for quality in the spirit. But bartenders who were born during those years are the ones who will show the world's fashion elite that Jimmy Choo's Tokyo opening doesn't have to be cheered on the roof of the world's most expensive property with imported Champagne. A celebration with Japanese whisky in tow might just be in order—perhaps mixed with an Asian pear.

MIZUWARI

Like all good Japanese edibles and potables, there is the traditional way
to drink whisky with water. It's a style of drink that can be made with
all sorts of hard liquor, but whisky makes the best version. It's full of
arbitrary tradition and mystical numbers. It's a simple drink, but must
be done perfectly to get it just right. It's a highball, or *mizuwari*: just
whisky and water. If you're investing a lot of money in a bottle of Japanese whisky, you might want to save this drink for a cheaper bottle. If
you decide to make it with an expensive single malt, it will be the best
mizuwari you'll ever drink.

Ice cubes
1 oz/30 ml blended Japanese whisky (anything you can get your hands on)
3 oz/90 ml water

Add a few pieces of ice to a tall glass. (There's some discussion as
to whether the ice should be in spheres or cubes, so just use what
you've got.) Pour in the whisky. Stir clockwise with deliberation
13½ times. Top up with more ice. Add the water and stir clockwise
slowly 3½ times, then serve.

NAIL IN THE COFFIN

Brian Means, San Francisco

This drink is a modern twist on the rusty nail. It's an intricate version of the cocktail that uses Japanese whisky instead of Scotch, Licor 43 instead of Drambuie, and some added flavors to make it a bit more complex. Brian told me he meant it to be enjoyed toward the end of a meal—to put the final nail in your coffin. And it's an impressive creation to wow your guests.

1½ oz/45 ml Yamazaki 12 single malt
¾ oz/25 ml Madeira (preferably Rainwater)
½ oz/15 ml Licor 43 (see note) or other vanilla liqueur
¼ oz/10 ml Fernet Branca
Ice cubes
Grated black cardamom pod, for garnish

Combine the whisky, Madeira, vanilla liqueur, and Fernet Branca in a mixing glass with ice and stir until well chilled, about 20 seconds. Strain into a chilled Nick and Nora glass or other cocktail glass. Garnish with the cardamom before serving.

NOTE: Licor 43 is a citrus-scented sweet liqueur flavored with vanilla. If you can't find it at the store, Bols vanilla brandy is easier to find and a good substitute.

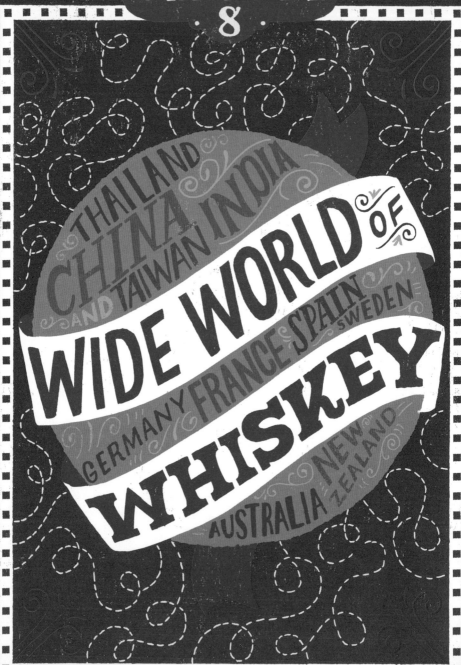

THAILAND CHINA AND TAIWAN INDIA

WIDE WORLD OF

GERMANY FRANCE SPAIN SWEDEN

WHISKEY

AUSTRALIA NEW ZEALAND

A generation ago, whiskey from anywhere but Scotland, Ireland, Canada, or the United States was generally regarded as a sick joke, not worthy of your money or your mouth. But the times they are a-changin' and our globe is getting smaller. Whiskey is becoming a universal phenomenon translated into languages on every continent. Exported, imported, and tasted from each end of the world, every province, and in bars in countries that you never knew existed, whiskey is now the worldliest of spirits. Its international appeal has made Goliaths out of alcohol companies and has continued to perpetuate an appetite to make homegrown whiskey in countries that had never before dreamed of it.

Like the fashion trends that were born in Tokyo and hit the rest of the world a decade later, Japan has set the pace. They proved that they could make whiskey and line up the bottles in competitions next to Scotch (and win). Now countries across the globe from Tanzania to Sweden are making whiskey, and thirsty consumers are taking note. The regional spread of whiskey making will be one of the lasting legacies of the coming decades.

The following is a simple whirlwind tour of the major players and important places to know about when you're out discovering new whiskey.

INDIA

With a population around 1.25 billion, India makes up the largest market of consumers of brown spirits in the world. Lasting cultural impacts from British colonialism have sent whisky cravings down through the ranks and have made it a staple cultural emblem. The British Empire's iron rule over colonial India was going on just about the same time that whisky in Scotland was booming and serving the British royal line. Fine Scotches were certainly sent to the English elite holding a tight grip on the "jewel in the British crown."

With a craving for whisky, homegrown Indian brands took on stereotypical Scottish names and identities, like **OFFICER'S CHOICE** and **BAGPIPER**. These brands sell ten times more bottles every year than there are people in Australia. However, since they are blends made from molasses and sugar, they technically aren't whiskies at all. In fact, the majority of bottles labeled "whisky" in India are some mix of malts, rum, brandy, and mystery spirits (often with whisky flavoring). Although they might not taste like any familiar Scotches, they are certainly blazing a deep path in the demand for whiskies. Vijay Mallya, the billionaire business mogul who owns several of the country's top alcohol brands, has also bought the Scottish distilleries **DALMORE** and **WHYTE & MACKAY**. Although high tariffs generally make Scotch difficult and expensive to import into India, many observers think this will soon change—or will have by the time you read this.

A couple of well-respected single malts are being bottled in India and are now available internationally. **AMRUT** makes the best known and its whiskies are gaining the attention of consumers who value quality Scotches. Named for the Sanskrit word for "immortal nectar," its barley is grown in Punjab in the foothills of the Himalayas. The company has been making whisky since the 1940s and created its first single malt in 2004. It's now exported widely and will be your best shot at trying (real) Indian whisky at the forefront of the industry.

CONTINENTAL EUROPE AND THE WHY NOT? FACTOR

With close proximity to the whisky heartland, mainland Europe has seen the growth of the industry in the last thirty years. Wales is now making whisky for the first time in 150 years, and both Germany and France have dozens of distilleries. Many of the European distilleries (and those around the world) follow a story similar to that of the Swedish whisky MACKMYRA. A group of friends got together for a skiing trip, and after finishing several bottles of single malt, they asked themselves why not? Why couldn't a whisky be made in Sweden or Switzerland or Spain? Soon enough the Swedish friends had built a distillery and were using local ingredients to make their Scotch-style single malts. MACKMYRA has already won a bushel of recognitions at both Stockholm and international competitions.

Many western and northern European countries are huge consumers of whiskies, and making a homespun version is helpful in filling a domestic need. A few of the European companies (including MACKMYRA) are already expanding internationally.

DOWN UNDER

The desire to drink domestic whisky and the dream to make it have driven the development of distilleries in continental Australia, Tasmania, and New Zealand. Many are using local barley, local peat, and local water. Distillers and entrepreneurs are realizing that temperatures across parts of the continent are perfect for aging whisky and some of the bottlings are quite tasty. A handful of these are making it around the world and can be tasted alongside your Scotches. The whiskies from LARK, a Tasmanian-based distillery, are among the most common to have made it abroad.

CHINA AND TAIWAN

With a population that exceeds India's by more than one hundred million, China's expanding middle class is quickly becoming the world's largest market primed to drink an unprecedented quantity of whiskey. Although the country doesn't share with India the same historical connection to Britain, China has a cultural infatuation with Western consumer goods that takes hold of everything from iPhones to Starbucks. Bottles of imported blended whiskey already grace top shelves of mega clubs and business bars from Beijing to Shanghai. They are splashed across billboards and poured by waiters in tuxedos and white gloves. It's not uncommon for consumers to drink extremely expensive bottles of whiskey with green tea, thus putting their own spin on a domestic drinking culture. Because the population currently drinks a ton of *baijiu*, a harsh-flavored distilled liquor typically made from sorghum, whiskey brings a smooth and high-class alternative. Knockoffs and fake bottles are sold on the black market, and Scotch is a status symbol that goes hand in hand with China's new wealth. **Although there is no legitimate whiskey being produced in China yet, a booming industry is sure to pop up in the next couple of decades to quench the thirst of 20 percent of the world's population.**

Taiwan's **KAVALAN** distillery is already tapping into China's market. After quickly establishing itself and selling its first bottle in 2008, it is already producing award-winning single malts. It has targeted its flavors toward the Asian market, focusing more on fruity, light styles instead of peaty, smoky whiskies. **KAVALAN**'s output is not an anomaly, but rather a forerunner in a new trend of whiskies that aren't served with a Scottish accent. Several tour guides in Scotland mentioned that Taiwanese tourists are coming out to the whisky capital in droves. The fire is spreading.

THAILAND

Although I've heard a lot about Thai whisky, the country doesn't actually make any. Brands like MEKHONG whisky are actually types of flavored rum made from sugar and rice. This is not to say that you shouldn't reach for a glass of it to do some "research" while you're visiting Bangkok, but it just doesn't fill the same niche as whiskies being produced elsewhere. I recommend you stay away from anything with snakes in it, too.

———————

This is not an exhaustive account of whiskey around the world. The technology for making high-quality spirits is replicable, and local ingredients or imports easily slide into recipes. Whiskey is no longer a spirit made only in Ireland and Scotland and imbibed by subjects of the royal crown. Neither do you need to speak English nor be a whiskey expert to start producing it. Pakistan even boasts a whisky made with local barley. Although 97 percent of the country can't legally drink it, and the product cannot be exported legally, it didn't stop some clever distillers from reappropriating an old British Raj brewery.

None of this is to say that whiskey making is easy. There's a reason that the best brands out there are generations into the art. **The coming decades of whiskey will bring us bar menus with a list of countries that looks like an attendance sheet for the United Nations.** Traveling will open up new flavor journeys into regional whiskies and malts that rival the GLENFIDDICHES and JOHNNIE WALKERS of the world. My great-grandchildren will probably read this book and have a good laugh that I neglected to include a chapter on Ghanaian whisky.

MALTING

FERMENT

GEEKING OUT

DISTILLATION

TO the BARREL

If you've found yourself on this page, you're thirsty for more, and you're a whiskey nerd (that's great!). Throughout the rest of the book, I've oversimplified the incredibly complex process of making whiskey. It's a dizzying production that takes years to understand and decades to master. Small intricacies of the process can tweak the end flavor and are manipulated by distillers around the world. Sometimes it's great to go a little deeper down the rabbit hole and learn more about the process of making whiskey and the production details of our favorite drinks and how to enjoy them. Here we go:

MALTING

Some grains used for whiskey are malted before they even get to the distillery. That means that they are soaked in water and tricked into thinking it is springtime. They start sprouting, as you might expect, and the germination is stopped by heating or smoking the grains (this is where the peaty flavors can come in). The process helps to prepare the starch in the grain and make it easier to access and convert to a sugary mix that is ideal for yeast to eat and then excrete alcohol. Traditionally, the malting process took place on floors of distilleries. Indeed, it's an incredible sight, the barley in hypnotic patterned mounds that stretch from wall to wall. Today, this arduous practice is continued in only a small handful of distilleries. The rest get their barley premalted from centralized malting houses.

GETTING TO FERMENTATION

Whether it is malted barley or heaps of corn, the grain arrives at distilleries by the truckload. It's ripped apart with machines and ground into flour (grist). The flour is combined with hot water and mixed in a process that converts the starches to sugars. The mixture, now called wort, is then cooled and married with yeast in perhaps one of the most important steps in the whole process. This combination starts the fermentation and gets the yeast gnawing on the sugars in the mash. Have you seen the term *sour mash* on your bottle of bourbon? That refers to using some of the leftovers from a previous fermentation (they look like polenta) and mixing them with the next batch of bourbon, like a sourdough starter.

If you recall the long equations from high-school chemistry class, you'll remember that what goes into the equation on the left side must come out on the other side. In this case, sugar (from the grain) and yeast go in and alcohol and carbon dioxide come out. The mash looks like it is boiling, but it is actually carbon dioxide bubbling off from the fermentation, which is also creating alcohol and heat. Fear not about global warming: carbon released into the environment in this process is offset by growing more barley, so we're good to go.

Sticking your head above one of these massive fermentation tanks is a daunting proposition. **Late stages of the fermentation leave little oxygen in the air above the vat, and taking a big whiff is like inhaling a punch in the face.** The length of the fermentation process will differ among distilleries, and longer fermentations can produce more fruity and acidic flavors. Even the material used for these tanks (wash backs) can affect the flavor of the final product. Many Scotch distilleries used to hire kids to beat down the bubbles formed by the fermentation process to prevent the concoction from overflowing. Now they've got mechanical arms that whip them into shape. When the fermentation process is completed and the yeast has died out, the liquid left behind is basically a warm, low-alcohol beer, known as distiller's beer in American distilleries and wash in European ones. It's a laxative and not tasty enough to serve up in a pint glass, but it does have a rich grain flavor and all the alcohol needed to make whiskey. The next step is distilling the beer to concentrate the alcohol and draw out the subtle flavors.

CONCENTRATING THE ALCOHOL

The beer is now moved from the fermentation tank to the still. In Scotland, only the liquid is taken, and the pieces of grain are left behind and fed to the local cattle. At TALISKER, since there aren't many cows, the nutrient-rich leftovers are pumped into the nearby bay, which in turn helps spawn incredible seafood. Once pumped into the still, the beer is boiled, and because alcohol boils at a lower temperature than water, the alcohol (as vapor) is captured on its way out and condensed in the iconic winding copper coil into a liquid that will become whiskey. This process is usually repeated for a second time to purify the spirit. Generally, in Irish distilleries (and a few distilleries elsewhere), the process is repeated a third time, creating an even lighter spirit and removing more of the "impurities" and heavier compounds (that is, flavors and aromatics). In vodkas and neutral grain spirits, this process is continued until the resulting alcohol crosses over the 94.8 percent alcohol threshold (when it's made), thus essentially eliminating any taste (that's the point in vodka). Many whiskey blends contain light alcohol that gets close to that line. Whereas the purity at that point is good for smooth vodka, it wipes out the taste and body of a whiskey.

When the alcohol comes out of the still, the distiller must take only the best section of the spirit. The first alcohol that comes out, known as heads, has methanol in it, a compound that is used for antifreeze and can kill you. Heard of people going blind from moonshine or other homemade alcohol? It's the heads that could do it. (Interestingly, one cure for methanol poisoning is ethanol, that is, the alcohol we drink. Your body ends up processing the booze and letting the methanol pass through.) The tails, or the end of the alcohol that comes off the still, is heavy in oils, flavors, and impurities that give a whiskey both deep and potentially bitter flavors and can give you more of a headache in the morning. It's the middle ethanol, or the heart, that will go on to be barreled and aged for later drinking.

As is the case with most modern distilleries, a lot of the process is done by computer and almost entirely automated. Distillery managers monitor what is going on where and can make adjustments along the way. They become so used to smells that they sense changes in aroma that might be issues in the process.

TO THE BARREL

Legal regulations guide distillers as to how strong a spirit can be when it's poured into a barrel for aging. To be legal, bourbon whiskey must be barreled at no more than 62.5 percent alcohol. Distillers can choose to barrel their bourbon at lower strengths, which can greatly impact the final flavors. The stronger the alcohol, the more flavor it will pull out from the wooden barrel. After distillation, the alcohol is usually much stronger than 62.5 percent alcohol, so distillers add water to get the desired alcohol content. Anywhere along the line it's perfectly legal for whiskey makers to add pure water. And they do.

Aging is both the most simple and most complex part of the process. The simple: distilleries put alcohol into barrels and wait for years to open it. The complicated: on the inside, the science of flavors is a complex chemical and sensory study that has taken years to understand. The liquor's interaction with the wood is a technical process in which flavors, colors, and oils are pulled out of the barrel. Make one mistake along the distilling process and it could be accentuated or resolved after years of aging. **BUFFALO TRACE** distillery has run a "single oak project" testing how different trees (and different parts of trees) affect the taste of its bourbon. They made barrels from pieces of a single tree (usually barrel boards come from any number of trees from any region), and it's noticeable that no two of the whiskies are the same.

As the whiskey ages, some of the liquid evaporates into the air, becoming the so-called angel's share. In more humid atmospheres, more of the water evaporates than alcohol, leaving a stronger whiskey than what was placed in the barrel. In drier, cooler climates like Scotland, the angels take more of the alcohol, leaving a spirit with a lowered alcohol level. Either way, it takes a large portion of the end product. In the United States, it amounts to between 2 and 6 percent annually. It makes older whiskey more expensive and leaves us with divine spirits.

TRICKS OF THE TRADE

Although nothing can really be added or taken out of most whiskies, a few exceptions and common tricks are used to produce a consistently uniform whiskey across hundreds of thousands of bottles. Scotch whisky makers are legally allowed to add caramel coloring to get the color just right. Since Scotch and other whiskies are aged in used barrels, the color of a whisky can differ greatly from batch to batch, depending on the quality of the wood. The ability to add color ensures that a bottle in New York will always look identical to a bottle in Paris.

If you've got an old bottle of whiskey and you hold it up to the light, you may see some residue in the bottle. Usually the dark matter is a mix of fatty acids, esters, and essential oils that is a by-product of the distilling process. Many companies clean out the residue by a system of chill filtration. To do this, distilleries cool down the whiskey to solidify the residue and then filter it (think coffee filter). It's done for aesthetic reasons (to stop a whiskey from clouding), though the process can dampen the flavor and aromatics. A burgeoning appetite for unfiltered whiskies is pushing along the trend, and some brands proudly mark it on the bottle. If you come across a bottle that has turned cloudy, don't stress about it. It's perfectly quaffable.

STILL READING?

Two types of stills are used in whiskey making. The first is the traditional and iconic copper pot still. The pot still is the famous one you've seen in beautiful distillery images: a big Hershey's Kiss—shaped copper bowl with a coil at the back. It's what most bootleggers were using during Prohibition, and it could have come straight out of Willy Wonka's factory. Pot stills produce alcohol of around 60 to 180 proof on a first run, depending on design and what alcohol you're starting with. Used for all single malts, most Irish whiskies, and across Japan, pot stills generally give spirits a deeper and richer mouthfeel because they retain many of the oils that give whiskey its flavor. Each distillery's pot stills are unique, and each little difference in their shape can affect the taste of the final product. Even the angle of the arm at the top of the still has a profound impact on the flavor profile.

Column stills, on the other hand, run continuously and can easily produce much higher-proof alcohol faster and more cheaply. Also known as the Coffey still after the Irishman who patented it in 1831, the continuous column still is a massive cylinder that can crank out alcohol nonstop. It is generally used for very strong spirits that are produced without rich flavors:

vodkas, gins, rums, and grain-neutral spirits (some of which find themselves in whiskey blends). Column stills are also used in a slightly different manner to produce most major bourbons.

When it comes to distilling, copper is the magical material. Originally used because it is a great heat conductor, the metal also strips out unfavorable sulfur compounds and releases esters (and some fruity notes with them) as it touches the new spirit. I've heard rumors that some distillers throw pennies in the bottom of noncopper column stills to re-create the effect. For fear of changing any flavors along the way, distilleries are extremely cautious about repairing or replacing any of their equipment. Often distilleries will replace only one piece of a still at a time, and only when completely necessary, to mitigate any possible changes in flavor.

FILLING THE GAPS WITH SCOTCH

In chapter 5, I broke down the kinds of Scotch whisky into single malts and blends. Although that's the easy black-and-white way to understand Scotch, there are a couple of other categories that are less common, though you do come across them every once in a while.

Single Grain

Yes, barley is a grain, but somewhere along the line, grain whisky came to mean any whisky that is not made from malted barley. Just seven grain-whisky distilleries currently exist in Scotland. They pump out massive quantities of light grain spirits and generally aren't open to visitors. Although grain whiskies serve as the base for larger blends, some higher-quality batches get bottled and carry the title "single grain" Scotch. As with single malts, the word *single* refers to a single distillery, but the whisky can be, and often is, made from a mix of grains. Single-grain whiskies are scarce in the world of Scotch and you'll have to seek them out. You'll rarely find them on the menu at your neighborhood bar.

Blended Grain

Since most grain whisky is cheap and used to make blends, it's rare to find grain whiskies blended together without some malted barley in the mix. But a handful of companies exist that blend a few single-grain whiskies from multiple distilleries without using malted barley. FAMOUS GROUSE puts out a very light blended-grain whisky called SNOW GROUSE that it recommends you leave in the freezer until it's "seriously chilled." Freezing booze usually mutes its flavors, so they are clearly shooting for a very different kind of whisky.

Blended Malt

If you create a blend with single malts and leave out the cheap light-grain whisky, you're left with a much different product. Rather than allow an individual single malt to dictate the taste of the whisky, blenders can pick and choose single malts from different distilleries to cook up a custom flavor. Although not as common as their single-malt counterparts, several independent bottling companies turn out some great blended malts. COMPASS BOX, one of the best-known producers, purchases casks and mixes them under its own labels. A few of the big brands have also made blended malts; JOHNNIE WALKER GREEN LABEL is one of them. Since these blenders can use Scotch from any distillery and have a much broader flavor range to work with, many of these whiskies are beautiful.

PUT YOUR GLASSES ON

There's a lot of talk about what glass to use when tasting whiskey, and it's a valid (if geeky) conversation. Just going for a drink? Use anything that holds liquid. If you're out to taste whiskey, the shape, material, and size of the glass will make a difference. You can easily do a test with some friends by putting the same whiskey into three differently shaped glasses to smell and taste how the shapes can affect the experience. A whiskey from a shot class will taste slightly differently from the same liquid in a wineglass or a whiskey snifter. Depending on its shape, the glass will hold the alcohol and aromas in distinctive ways, and because smell is a large part of how we taste, the glass affects the entire whiskey experience.

In general, your best choice is a tulip-shaped glass designed specifically for whiskey tasting. It will help to concentrate the aromas precisely where you stick your nose into the glass. Think of glassware as a prism. If you shoot a white light through a great prism, a rainbow of colors will come out the other end. Similarly, you want to be able to taste the rainbow and the different flavors from a whiskey. One of the hottest glasses right now is the Glencairn glass. First sold in 2001, it was designed for ideal tasting, smelling, and all-around fanciful swagger. You surely don't need to go out and buy a new set of crystal glasses to appreciate a fine whiskey, but sometimes plastic cups just won't cut it.

———————

This is just the tip of the iceberg. If you are craving more information, it is not difficult to find. Head to a distillery to see all of this in action. The world knows no limit on geeking out when it comes to whiskey. You'll always have company, and the Internet will bring you seconds away from millions of others who are just as eager to obsess about whiskey as you are.

CHEAT SHEET

ABV. The percentage of alcohol in a bottle. The acronym stands for "alcohol by volume," and the strength of the alcohol can change the way a whiskey tastes and how it feels going down your throat. By no means is it the most important thing when drinking whiskey, unless you have a meeting afterward.

AGING. The process of holding a whiskey in an oak barrel for a period of time. Aging in wood mellows a whiskey's harsh alcohol and gives it its dark color and many of its burnt, vanilla, and caramel flavors. Bourbon and most American whiskies are aged in new barrels that have been charred on the inside. In Scotland, the whisky often rests in barrels that were previously used to age bourbon, wines, or other spirits.

AMERICAN WHISKEY. This is whiskey made anywhere in the United States. Depending on its ingredients, it can be classified as bourbon or rye, but it doesn't have to be. There are plenty of bottles that are just labeled "blended American whiskey." Knowing the four terms that follow will make you better poised to order an American whiskey you'll enjoy.

bottled in bond or bonded. Whiskey distilled in one year, by one distiller, at one distillery. Must also be 100 proof.

bourbon. American whiskey made from 51 percent or more corn and aged in charred new American oak barrels. It must be at least 80 proof.

rye. Made from at least 51 percent rye and following the same rules that apply to bourbon making.

straight. A quality marker for any American whiskey that signifies that it is made from 51 percent or more of a single grain, it was aged for at least two years in charred new oak barrels, and only water has been added to the mix.

ANGEL'S SHARE. A mix of water and alcohol that evaporates from whiskey as it ages (at a rate of 2 to 6 percent per year, depending on atmospheric conditions where the whiskey is aging). This helps to make older whiskies rarer and more costly. As the evaporating alcohol escapes into the air, it spawns the growth of a black fungus around the distilling site, a telltale sign that proved the downfall of many bootleggers during Prohibition.

BOOTLEGGER. A person who makes, sells, or transports alcohol illegally. Bootlegging was a common job during Prohibition, and the classic booze of the bootlegger was moonshine.

CANADIAN WHISKY. Whisky made in Canada, which is usually a blend and fairly light and easy to drink. In Canada, the term *rye* is synonymous with whisky.

CASK STRENGTH. Aged whiskey just out of the barrel, with no water added by the distiller. It is generally 50 to 60 percent alcohol.

CHILL FILTRATION. *See* filtration.

DISTILLATION. The process of boiling an alcoholic mixture and condensing the resulting vapor to make a concentrated alcohol. All whiskey is essentially distilled beer.

DRAM. Once a unit of measurement in apothecaries, dram is now just slang for a wee bit of whiskey. It would be the same as saying a glass of whiskey. Get together with your friends for a dram or two or three. It's the perfect amount.

FERMENTATION. The wonderful natural process that makes booze. It happens when yeast eats sugar and shits out alcohol. Carbon dioxide is also a by-product of the process.

Grains are mixed with water and yeast to get the fermentation process going. The end result is basically warm beer. But trust me, you wouldn't want to drink it. All whiskey starts out like this.

FILTRATION. A method used to make a whiskey more "pure." There are a handful of different filtering methods, many of which are not allowed in the making of most whiskies. The most notable is chill filtration, in which whiskey is chilled so that impurities will solidify and can be strained out, thus preventing the whiskey from turning cloudy in the bottle. Many connoisseurs will tell you that chill filtration takes out some of the flavors and aromas along with the haze. If your whiskey does get cloudy, don't worry about it. It's just a question of aesthetics and will taste fine.

HOW TO DRINK WHISKEY. Any way you want.

HOW TO DRINK *MORE* WHISKEY. Please read this book again.

IRISH WHISKEY. Whiskey made in Ireland, which typically lacks that smoky, peated flavor of Scotch. It is usually distilled three times, a process that often yields a lighter whiskey—key to a night of heavy partying and drinking. Of course, as with any whiskey category, there are whiskies that break the rules. Jameson is the most common, but others are out there.

JAPANESE WHISKY. Whisky made in Japan, which tastes more like Scotch whisky than any other type.

MALT. Malt refers to malted (germinated) barley and is also a nickname for single malts. Barley is malted by soaking it in water and allowing it to sprout. It is then heated (or smoked) to stop it from growing into full plants. Malting makes barley the perfect ingredient for whiskey.

MASHBILL. The amount of each kind of grain in a whiskey—essentially the recipe. This is a geeky term that shows everyone around you that you know what the hell you are talking about. The appropriate way to use the term in a sentence is "What is this whiskey's mashbill?"

MOIST AND DRY COUNTIES. Dry counties (in the United States) do not sell any alcohol within their limits. Moist counties allow some restricted sale of alcohol, often to appease businesses and allow for an added tax source. Many moist counties in Tennessee allow for the sale of alcohol in establishments that also sell food.

MOONSHINE. Historically, moonshine was the unaged whiskey made illegally during Prohibition. It was said to have been made under the shine of the moon, away from the authorities. The term is being reclaimed, and you can buy a bottle of unaged whiskey, or white dog (see page 29), that is marketed as moonshine.

NEAT. Any alcohol served solo. No cola, no juice, no water, and no ice. It's a great way to taste a whiskey because there's nothing to interfere with its true flavor.

NOSE. As a noun, the nose is the aroma of the whiskey. It's the smart way to tell someone of its scent. As a verb, it means to smell your whiskey. Although it might sound cocky, it's totally fine to say something like, "I'm getting a bit of star anise on the nose of this Scotch."

PEAT. Decayed vegetation that is rich in energy (it's an important source of cooking and heating fuel in some places). Peat is used to smoke the barley that ultimately gives Scotch its famous smoky taste.

PROHIBITION. The shameful era in the United States between 1920 and 1933 during which alcohol was illegal. It was illegal to buy, sell, or make booze except for small quantities for religious (and sometimes medicinal) purposes. The thirteen years decimated the American whiskey industry and palate. The country is just now finally getting up to speed with the rest of the world.

PROOF. Double the percentage of alcohol in a whiskey. The proof has become a common way to discuss the alcoholic strength of a spirit. As the story goes, the word came from sailors who would douse gunpowder with rum to test the strength of the booze. If the gunpowder exploded, it was proof that the rum was strong. If it didn't ignite, they knew it was watered down and not fit for drinking.

PURE POT STILL WHISKEY. Also known as single pot still whiskey, a style of whiskey produced by Irish distillers made by mixing together malted and unmalted barley. Pure pot still whiskies must come from a single distillery, and although they are delicious, you won't find a lot of them on the market.

SCOTCH WHISKY. Whisky made in Scotland, which is usually distilled twice and always aged in second-hand barrels. Scotch often has a distinctive smoky, or peaty, flavor due to the use of malted barley that has been smoked over a peat fire. In a Scottish bar, you always ask for whisky, not Scotch.

SINGLE BARREL. Whiskey bottled from only one barrel. The term can be used for any kind of whiskey, anywhere in the world. If you like what you are drinking, look for the specific barrel number on your bottle and see if you can go get another bottle from the same barrel. The taste of single-barrel whiskies can differ from bottle to bottle. Since they are hand chosen, they are higher end—both in flavor and in price.

SINGLE MALT. Whiskey made entirely from malted barley at one distillery. Although single malts can be made anywhere in the world, more often than not they are single malts from Scotland.

SMALL BATCH. A brilliant marketing term. It is a self-bestowed title on whiskey that is made or bottled in small batches. Smaller than what? The issue, of course, is that there is no measuring stick for "small." Usually it's a brand's premium or special label, and considerable care goes into choosing which barrels to bottle in the small batch. The price reflects this special attention.

SOUR MASH. The leftover grain mash from fermenting that is thrown back into the fermenting vat to help start the fermentation process all over again for the next batch. It is a common practice in the bourbon industry and is akin to the "starter" for sourdough bread or kombucha.

STILL. The large contraption that boils the fermented beer to create concentrated alcohol (whiskey). There are column stills (industrial and efficient) and pot stills (usually made from copper and shaped like a Hershey's Kiss). Most bourbons are made in column stills and most single malts are made in pot stills.

WHISKEY. A distilled spirit that can be made from a single grain or any mix of different cereal grains, including corn, barley, wheat, rye, or spelt. It needs to at least touch oak, but there is no specific age requirement for whiskies in general.

WHISKEY REBELLION. America's first uprising (1794) of Western pioneers protesting against a new tax on whiskey. They were still fighting off the memory of taxation imposed by the British and felt that the tax unfairly hurt those living on the western frontier (because they made more whiskey).

WHISKEY STONES. Literally rocks, these stones are often made of soapstone. They are kept in the freezer and dropped into a glass of whiskey to chill it without diluting it. If you want to be a die-hard fan, go to your favorite distillery, pick up a couple of stones from the surrounding grounds, wash them, freeze them, and then toss them into your drink. You're not going to find whiskey stones at the local bar, but they are a great way to drink whiskey neat and cold without keeping the bottle in the freezer like a freshman in college.

WHITE DOG. Also known as white whiskey and in the United Kingdom as new make, white dog is the clear unaged spirit that comes off the still. It's strong and tastes quite a bit like the grain from which it was made. When it's made illegally in the United States, it's called moonshine.

SELECTED BIBLIOGRAPHY AND RESOURCES

Allhoff, Fritz, and Marcus P. Adams. *Whiskey & Philosophy: A Small Batch of Spirited Ideas*. Hoboken, NJ: John Wiley & Sons, 2010.

Brown, Lorraine. *200 Years of Tradition: The Story of Canadian Whisky*. Markham, Ont.: Fitzhenry & Whiteside, 1994.

Bunting, Chris. Nonjatta blog. nonjatta.blogspot.com.

De Kergommeaux, Davin. *Canadian Whisky: The Portable Expert*. Toronto: McClelland & Stewart, 2012.

Downard, William L. *Dictionary of the History of the American Brewing and Distilling Industries*. Westport, CT: Greenwood, 1980.

Gabányi, Stefan. *Whisk(e)y*. New York: Abbeville, 1997.

Jackson, Michael, and Dave Broom. *Whiskey: The Definitive World Guide*. New York: DK, 2005.

Jew, Chris, and Nate Nicoll. The Whisky Wall blog. whiskywall.com.

Lubbers, Bernie. *Bourbon Whiskey: Our Native Spirit*. Indianapolis: Blue River, 2011.

MacLean, Charles. *Whisky*. London: DK, 2008.

———. *World Whiskey*. New York: DK, 2009.

Murray, Jim. *Jim Murray's Whiskey Bible*. London: Carlton, 2003.

Peck, Garrett. *The Prohibition Hangover: Alcohol in America from Demon Rum to Cult Cabernet*. New Brunswick, NJ: Rutgers University Press, 2009.

Rannie, William F. *Canadian Whisky: The Product and the Industry*. Lincoln, Ont.: W. F. Rannie, 1976.

Watman, Max. *Chasing the White Dog: An Amateur Outlaw's Adventures in Moonshine*. New York: Simon & Schuster, 2011 (pbk. ed.).

Young, Al. *Four Roses: The Return of a Whiskey Legend*. Louisville, KY: Butler, 2010.

ACKNOWLEDGMENTS

Many thanks go to:

Victoria Gutierrez

Chris Jew & Nate Nicoll (WhiskyWall)

Chris Bunting

Allegra Ben-Amotz

John Jeffery

Ken Walczak

Davin de Kergommeaux

Samir Osman

The drunken lout who sat next to me at the Brazen Head

Carly Jansen

Ichiro Akuto

Kara Newman

Chris Jordan

Andie Ferman

Dave Smith!

Lance Winters

Alex Conway

Neyah White

The ridiculously wonderful folks at St. George Distillery

Bernie Lubbers

Dave Pudlo

Deanna Killackey

Aman Ahuja

Stephen Beal

Mitch Spierer

Craig Edelman

Eriq Wities

Sangita (for all of your patience and love)

Jonathan

Mom and Dad

My editors Lorena Jones and Amy Treadwell

And everyone else who helped along this journey.

INDEX